Presented To:

_____

_____

From:

_____

_____

Date:

_____

Thomas Nelson's
Children's
STORY
BIBLE

Thomas Nelson's
Children's
STORY
BIBLE

Illustrated By

NATALIE CARABETTA

NKJV

NEW KING JAMES VERSION®

Build Your Life On It.™

NELSON BIBLES
A Division of Thomas Nelson Publishers
Since 1798

Children's Story Bible
Table of Contents

EXPLORE THE BIBLE

Teach me, O Lord, the way of Your statutes, and I shall keep
it to the end. Give me understanding and I shall keep Your
law; indeed, I shall observe it with my whole heart.

—Psalm 119:33–34

Congratulations! You're old enough to graduate to a Bible for adults. When you were younger you might have read retold stories, but in this book you will be reading actual text from the New King James Version® (NKJV) of the Bible. And as you'll find out, the Bible tells about the creation of the world and the adventures of God's people over many centuries!

We've included three more things at the end of each story to help you as you explore what you have read:

> **DISCOVER:**
> where you answer questions (the answers are in the related story).
>
> **UNDERSTAND:**
> where a key word or concept in the story is explained.
>
> **LIVE IT OUT:**
> where you can apply the story to your everyday life.

There is also a Bible verse to challenge your memory skills.

This story book will help you begin your exploration of the Bible, and understanding the Bible will help you build a stronger personal relationship with God. As that relationship grows, you'll want to read more about these and other Bible stories!

God Creates Man, Woman, and Animals

Genesis 1:24–2:1

MEMORY VERSE:
In the beginning God created the heavens and the earth.

—Genesis 1:1

1...²⁴Then God said, "Let the earth bring forth the living creature according to its kind: cattle and creeping thing and beast of the earth, each according to its kind"; and it was so. ²⁵And God made the beast of the earth according to its kind, cattle according to its kind, and everything that creeps on the earth according to its kind. And God saw that it was good.

²⁶Then God said, "Let Us make man in Our image, according to Our likeness; let them have dominion over the fish of the sea, over the birds of the air, and over the cattle, over all the earth and over every creeping thing that creeps on the earth." ²⁷So God created man in His own image; in the image of God He created him; male and female He created them. ²⁸Then God blessed them, and God said to them, "Be fruitful and multiply; fill the earth and subdue it; have dominion over the fish of the sea, over the birds of the air, and over every living thing that moves on the earth."

²⁹And God said, "See, I have given you every herb that yields seed which is on the face of all the earth, and every tree whose fruit yields seed; to you it shall be for food. ³⁰Also, to every beast of the earth, to every bird of the air, and to everything that creeps on the earth, in which there is life, I have given every green herb for food"; and it was so. ³¹Then God saw everything that He had made, and indeed it was very good. So the evening and the morning were the sixth day.

2Thus the heavens and the earth, and all the host of them, were finished.

DISCOVER:

God made *all* the animals in the world in only one day.
What did God give the animals to eat?

UNDERSTAND:

Image is like an exact copy. Creating is like building.
So God built man like Himself.

LIVE IT OUT:

God has given us everything we need to follow in
His footsteps.

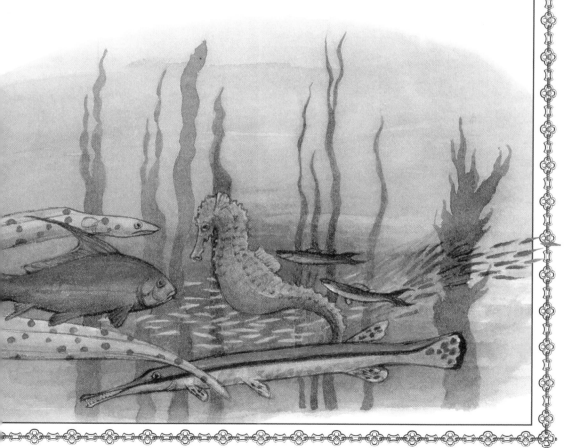

THE DECEITFUL SERPENT

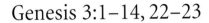

Genesis 3:1–14, 22–23

MEMORY VERSE:
Let no one deceive you with empty words, for because of these things the wrath of God comes upon the sons of disobedience.

—*Ephesians 5:6*

3 Now the serpent was more cunning than any beast of the field which the LORD God had made. And he said to the woman, "Has God indeed said, 'You shall not eat of every tree of the garden'?"

²And the woman said to the serpent, "We may eat the fruit of the trees of the garden; ³but of the fruit of the tree which is in the midst of the garden, God has said, 'You shall not eat it, nor shall you touch it, lest you die.'"

⁴Then the serpent said to the woman, "You will not surely die." ⁵For God knows that in the day you eat of it your eyes will be opened, and you will be like God, knowing good and evil."

6So when the woman saw that the tree was good for food, that it was pleasant to the eyes, and a tree desirable to make one wise, she took of its fruit and ate. She also gave to her husband with her, and he ate. 7Then the eyes of both of them were opened, and they knew that they were naked; and they sewed fig leaves together and made themselves coverings.

⁸And they heard the sound of the Lᴏʀᴅ God walking in the garden in the cool of the day, and Adam and his wife hid themselves from the presence of the Lᴏʀᴅ God among the trees of the garden.

⁹Then the Lᴏʀᴅ God called to Adam and said to him, "Where are you?"

¹⁰So he said, "I heard Your voice in the garden, and I was afraid because I was naked; and I hid myself."

¹¹And He said, "Who told you that you were naked? Have you eaten from the tree of which I commanded you that you should not eat?"

¹²Then the man said, "The woman whom You gave to be with me, she gave me of the tree, and I ate."

¹³And the Lᴏʀᴅ God said to the woman, "What is this you have done?"

The woman said, "The serpent deceived me, and I ate."

¹⁴So the Lᴏʀᴅ God said to the serpent: "Because you have done this, you are cursed more than all cattle and more than every beast of the field; on your belly you should go, and you shall eat dust all the days of your life . . ."

²²Then the L<small>ORD</small> God said, "Behold, the man has become like one of Us, to know good and evil. And now, lest he put out his hand and take also of the tree of life, and eat, and live forever"— ²³therefore the L<small>ORD</small> God sent him out of the garden of Eden to till the ground from which he was taken.

DISCOVER:
What did Adam and Eve do that was wrong? What did God do to punish the serpent?

UNDERSTAND:
A serpent is a snake. It tricked Eve into eating fruit from the forbidden tree.

LIVE IT OUT:
There will always be temptations. We must be careful of those who would like to see us do sinful things.

The Jealous Brother

Genesis 4:1–15

MEMORY VERSE:
But do not forget to do good and to share, for with
such sacrifices God is well pleased.

—*Hebrews 13:16*

4 Now Adam knew Eve his wife, and she conceived and bore Cain, and said, "I have acquired a man from the Lord." ²Then she bore again, this time his brother Abel. Now Abel was a keeper of sheep, but Cain was a tiller of the ground. ³And in the process of time it came to pass that Cain brought an offering of the fruit of the ground to the Lord. ⁴Abel also brought of the first-born of his flock and of their fat. And the Lord respected Abel and his offering,

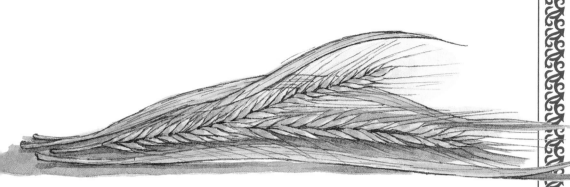

⁵but He did not respect Cain and his offering. And Cain was very angry, and his countenance fell.

⁶So the LORD said to Cain, "Why are you angry? And why has your countenance fallen? ⁷If you do well, will you not be accepted? And if you do not do well, sin lies at the door. And its desire is for you, but you should rule over it."

⁸Now Cain talked with Abel his brother; and it came to pass, when they were in the field, that Cain rose up against Abel his brother and killed him.

⁹Then the LORD said to Cain, "Where is Abel your brother?"

He said, "I do not know. Am I my brother's keeper?"

¹⁰And He said, "What have you done? The voice of your brother's blood cries out to Me from the ground. ¹¹So now you are cursed from the earth, which has opened its mouth to receive your brother's blood from your hand. ¹²When you till the ground, it shall no longer yield its strength to you. A fugitive and a vagabond you shall be on the earth."

¹³And Cain said to the LORD, "My punishment is greater than I can bear! ¹⁴Surely You have driven me out this day from the face of the ground; I shall be hidden from Your face; I shall be a fugitive and a vagabond on the earth, and it will happen that anyone who finds me will kill me."

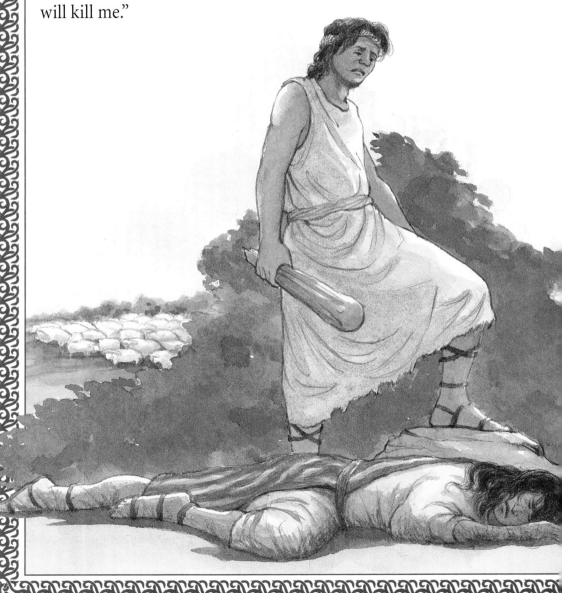

¹⁵And the Lord said to him, "Therefore, whoever kills Cain, vengeance shall be taken on him sevenfold." And the Lord set a mark on Cain, lest anyone finding him should kill him

DISCOVER:

Do you think Cain was jealous of his brother Abel? What did Cain do to Abel?

UNDERSTAND:

A vagabond is a person with no home who wanders from place to place. A fugitive is a person who runs away.

LIVE IT OUT:

Our heavenly Father makes sure we have a home with Him. God's people do not have to wander from place to place looking for safety.

NOAH BUILDS THE ARK

Genesis 6:5–8, 13–22

MEMORY VERSE:
For by grace you have been saved through faith, and
that not of yourselves; it is the gift of God....

—Ephesians 2:8

6...⁵Then the LORD saw that the wickedness of
man was great in the earth, and that every
intent of the thoughts of his heart was
only evil continually. ⁶And the LORD
was sorry that He had made man on the
earth, and He was grieved in His heart. ⁷So
the LORD said, "I will destroy man whom I
have created from the face of the earth, both
man and beast, creeping thing and birds of
the air, for I am sorry that I have made
them." ⁸But Noah found grace in the eyes of
the LORD....

¹³And God said to Noah, "The end of all
flesh has come before Me, for the earth is
filled with violence through them; and
behold, I will destroy them with the earth.
¹⁴Make yourself an ark of gopherwood;

make rooms in the ark, and cover it inside and outside with pitch. [15]And this is how you shall make it: The length of the ark shall be three hundred cubits, its width fifty cubits, and its height thirty cubits. [16]You shall make a window for the ark, and you shall finish it to a cubit from above; and set the door of the ark in its side. You shall make it with lower, second, and third decks.

17And behold, I Myself am bringing floodwaters on the earth, to destroy from under heaven all flesh in which is the breath of life; everything that is on the earth shall die. 18But I will establish My covenant with you; and you shall go into the ark—you, your sons, your wife, and your sons' wives with you. 19And of every living thing of all flesh you shall bring two of every sort into the ark, to keep them alive with you; they shall be male and female. 20Of the birds after their kind, of animals after their kind, and of every creeping thing of the earth after its kind, two of every kind will come to you to keep them alive. 21And you shall take for yourself of all food that is eaten, and you shall gather it to yourself; and it shall be food for you and for them."

22Thus Noah did; according to all that God commanded him, so he did.

DISCOVER:

Why did the Lord want to destroy the earth? Was it because He saw evil and was grieved because people were so wicked?

UNDERSTAND:

The name Noah means "rest" or "relief."

LIVE IT OUT:

Noah did all the Lord commanded him to do. Do you follow the Lord's commandments?

Noah and the Great Flood

Genesis 7:1–10, 12–17, 23–24

7Then the LORD said to Noah, "Come into the ark, you and all your household, because I have seen that you are righteous before Me in this generation. 2You shall take with you seven each of every clean animal, a male and his female; two each of animals that are unclean, a male and his female; 3also seven each of birds of the air, male and female, to keep the species alive on the face of all the earth. 4For after seven more days I will cause it to rain on the earth forty days and forty nights, and I will destroy from the face of the earth all living things that I have made." 5And Noah did according to all that the LORD commanded him. 6Noah was six hundred years old when the floodwaters were on the earth.

7So Noah, with his sons, his wife, and his sons' wives, went into the ark because of the waters of the flood. 8Of clean animals, of animals that are unclean, of birds, and of everything that creeps on the earth, 9two by two they went into the ark to Noah, male and female, as God had commanded Noah. 10And it came to pass after seven days that the waters of the flood were on the earth.... 12And the rain was on the earth forty days and forty nights.

13On the very same day Noah and Noah's sons, Shem, Ham, and Japheth, and Noah's wife and the three wives of his sons with them, entered the ark— 14they and every beast after its kind, all cattle after their kind, every creeping thing that creeps on the earth after its kind, and every bird after its kind, every bird of every sort. 15And they went into the ark to Noah, two by two, of all flesh in which is the breath of life. 16So those that entered, male and female of all flesh, went in as God had commanded him; and the LORD shut him in.

17Now the flood was on the earth forty days. The waters increased and lifted up the ark, and it rose high above the earth. . . .

23So He destroyed all living things which were on the face of the ground: both man and cattle, creeping thing and bird of the air. They were destroyed from the earth. Only Noah and those who were with him in the ark remained alive. 24And the waters prevailed on the earth one hundred and fifty days.

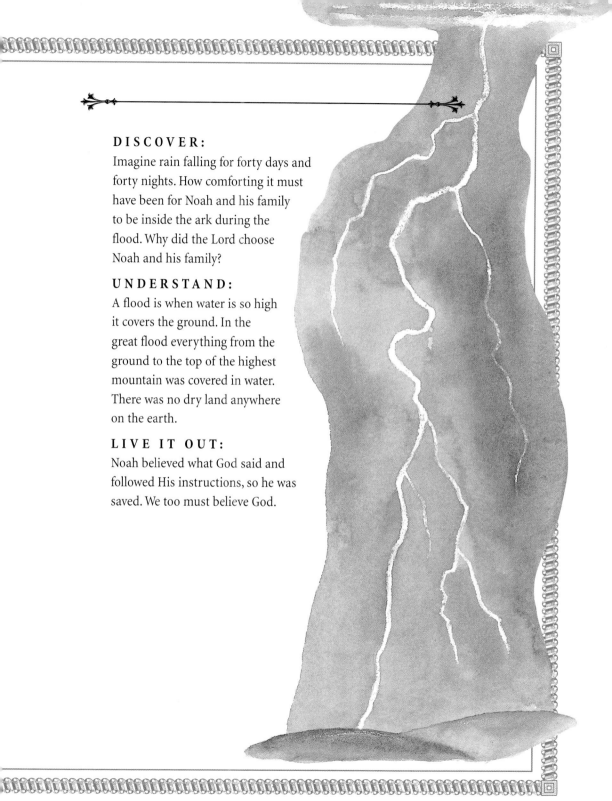

DISCOVER:

Imagine rain falling for forty days and forty nights. How comforting it must have been for Noah and his family to be inside the ark during the flood. Why did the Lord choose Noah and his family?

UNDERSTAND:

A flood is when water is so high it covers the ground. In the great flood everything from the ground to the top of the highest mountain was covered in water. There was no dry land anywhere on the earth.

LIVE IT OUT:

Noah believed what God said and followed His instructions, so he was saved. We too must believe God.

GOD'S RAINBOW PROMISE

Genesis 9:1–16

MEMORY VERSE:
"I set My rainbow in the cloud, and it shall be for the sign
of the covenant between Me and the earth."

—Genesis 9:13

9 So God blessed Noah and his sons, and said to them: "Be fruitful and multiply, and fill the earth. ²And the fear of you and the dread of you shall be on every beast of the earth, on every bird of the air, on all that move on the earth, and on all the fish of the sea. They are given into your hand. ³Every moving thing that lives shall be food for you. I have given you all things, even as the green herbs. ⁴But you shall not eat flesh with its life, that is, its blood. ⁵Surely for your lifeblood I will demand a reckoning; from the hand of every beast I will require it, and from the hand of man. From the hand of every man's brother I will require the life of man.

⁶"Whoever sheds man's blood, by man his blood shall be shed; for in the image of God He made man. ⁷And as for you, be fruitful and multiply; bring forth abundantly in the earth and multiply in it."

8Then God spoke to Noah and to his sons with him, saying:
9"And as for Me, behold, I establish My covenant with you and with
your descendants after you, 10and with every living creature that is
with you: the birds, the cattle, and every beast of the earth with you,
of all that go out of the ark, every beast of the earth. 11Thus I establish
My covenant with you: Never again shall all flesh be cut off by the
waters of the flood; never again shall there be a flood to destroy
the earth."

¹²And God said: "This is the sign of the covenant which I make between Me and you, and every living creature that is with you, for perpetual generations: ¹³I set My rainbow in the cloud, and it shall be for the sign of the covenant between Me and the earth. ¹⁴It shall be, when I bring a cloud over the earth, that the rainbow shall be seen in the cloud; ¹⁵and I will remember My covenant which is between Me and you and every living creature of all flesh; the waters shall never again become a flood to destroy all flesh. ¹⁶The rainbow shall be in the cloud, and I will look on it to remember the everlasting covenant between God and every living creature of all flesh that is on

DISCOVER:

When God put the rainbow in the sky, it was a sign of a covenant between God and all the people on the earth.

UNDERSTAND:

A covenant is a promise or an agreement. In this story about the rainbow, God promised to never again destroy the earth with a flood.

LIVE IT OUT:

We should be grateful to God, and do our best to obey and serve Him.

ABRAHAM LOOKS AT THE STARS

Genesis 15:5

MEMORY VERSE:

For when God made a promise to Abraham, because He could swear by no one greater, He swore by Himself, saying, "Surely blessing I will bless you, and multiplying I will multiply you."

—*Hebrews 6:13–14*

15…⁵Then He brought him outside and said, "Look now toward heaven, and count the stars if you are able to number them." And He said to him, "So shall your descendants be."

DISCOVER:

God made a covenant with Abraham. He promised to bless Abraham with land and many descendants.

UNDERSTAND:

Descendants are a person's children, grandchildren, great-grandchildren. God told Abraham he would have as many descendants as there are stars in the sky. Can you imagine having as many relatives as there are stars in the sky?

LIVE IT OUT:

God keeps all His promises. When we make promises, we should keep them too.

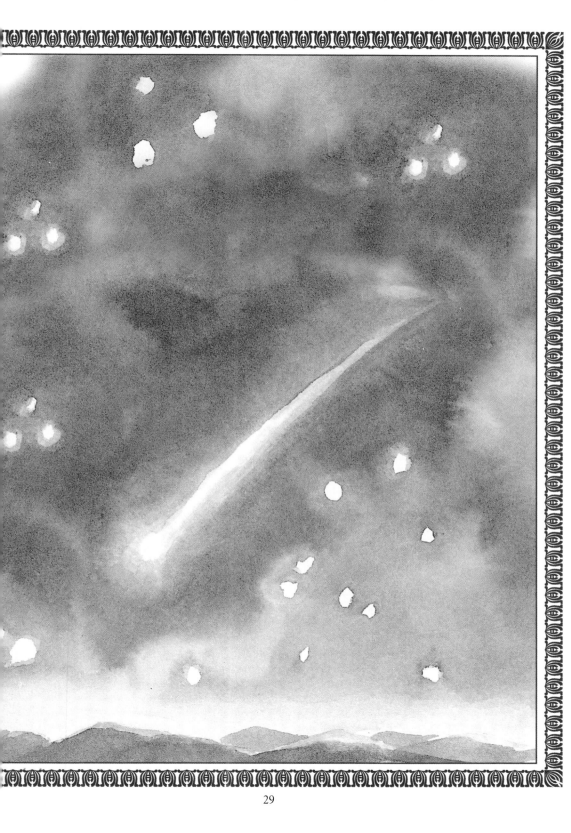

THE WICKED CITIES

Genesis 19:1–4, 15–17, 23–26

MEMORY VERSE:
A good man obtains favor from the LORD, but a man of
wicked intentions He will condemn.

—*Proverbs 12:2*

19 Now the two angels came to Sodom in the evening, and Lot was sitting in the gate of Sodom. When Lot saw them, he rose to meet them, and he bowed himself with his face toward the ground. 2And he said, "Here now, my lords, please turn in to your servant's house and spend the night, and wash your feet; then you may rise early and go on your way."

And they said, "No, but we will spend the night in the open square."

3But he insisted strongly; so they turned in to him and entered his house. Then he made them a feast, and baked unleavened bread, and they ate.

4Now before they lay down, the men of the city, the men of Sodom, both old and young, all the people from every quarter, surrounded the house. . . .

Lot went out to speak to the men. The mob tried to break down the door and enter Lot's house, but the two angels inside pulled Lot back into the house and shut the door. Then the angels struck the mob outside with blindness so they couldn't find the door. When the mob finally gave up and left, the angels told Lot to gather his family and leave the city, because the Lord had sent them to destroy the city.

15When the morning dawned, the angels urged Lot to hurry, saying, "Arise, take your wife and your two daughters who are here, lest you be consumed in the punishment of the city." 16And while he lingered, the men took hold of his hand, his wife's hand, and the hands of his two daughters, the LORD being merciful to him, and they brought him out and set him outside the city. 17So it came to pass, when they had brought them outside, that he said, "Escape for your life! Do not look behind you nor stay anywhere in the plain. Escape to the mountains, lest you be destroyed." . . .

But Lot was afraid to flee to the mountains, and asked for mercy. Again, the angels showed Lot mercy. They agreed not to destroy the small city of Zoar, and allowed Lot and his family to escape to Zoar instead of the mountains.

²³The sun had risen upon the earth when Lot entered Zoar. ²⁴Then the LORD rained brimstone and fire on Sodom and Gomorrah, from the LORD out of the heavens. ²⁵So He overthrew those cities, all the plain, all the inhabitants of the cities, and what grew on the ground.

²⁶But his [*Lot's*] wife looked back behind him, and she became a pillar of salt.

DISCOVER:
Lot and his daughters were saved when the cities of Sodom and Gomorrah were destroyed. Why was Lot's wife turned into a pillar of salt?

UNDERSTAND:
The men of Sodom and Gomorrah were wicked and sinful against God. But God showed Lot mercy and sent two angels to lead Lot and his family out of danger.

LIVE IT OUT:
The Lord is pleased with those who obey Him. We should always avoid evil.

ESAU SELLS HIS BIRTHRIGHT TO JACOB

Genesis 25:19–34

MEMORY VERSE:
Blessed is the nation whose God is the LORD, the people He
has chosen as His own inheritance.

—*Psalm 33:12*

25 ... ¹⁹This is the genealogy of Isaac, Abraham's son. Abraham begot Isaac. ²⁰Isaac was forty years old when he took Rebekah as wife, the daughter of Bethuel the Syrian of Padan Aram, the sister of Laban the Syrian. ²¹Now Isaac pleaded with the LORD for his wife, because she was barren; and the LORD granted his plea, and Rebekah his wife conceived. ²²But the children struggled together within her; and she said, "If all is well, why am I like this?" So she went to inquire of the LORD.

²³And the LORD said to her: "Two nations are in your womb, two peoples shall be separated from your body; one people shall be stronger than the other, and the older shall serve the younger."

²⁴So when her days were fulfilled for her to give birth, indeed there were twins in her womb. ²⁵And the first came out red. He was like a hairy garment all over; so they called his name Esau. ²⁶Afterward his brother came out, and his hand took hold of Esau's heel; so his name was called Jacob. Isaac was sixty years old when she bore them.

^{27}So the boys grew. And Esau was a skillful hunter, a man of the field; but Jacob was a mild man, dwelling in tents. ^{28}And Isaac loved Esau because he ate of his game, but Rebekah loved Jacob.

²⁹Now Jacob cooked a stew; and Esau came in from the field, and he was weary. ³⁰And Esau said to Jacob, "Please feed me with that same red stew, for I am weary." Therefore his name was called Edom.

³¹But Jacob said, "Sell me your birthright as of this day."

³²And Esau said, "Look, I am about to die; so what is this birthright to me?"

³³Then Jacob said, "Swear to me as of this day."

So he swore to him, and sold his birthright to Jacob. ³⁴And Jacob gave Esau bread and stew of lentils; then he ate and drank, arose, and went his way. Thus Esau despised his birthright.

DISCOVER:

In Bible times the firstborn son would inherit more of the father's property. It was called a "birthright."

UNDERSTAND:

Which son was born first, Esau or Jacob? What did Esau get in exchange for selling his birthright to Jacob?

LIVE IT OUT:

As children of God, our birthright (or inheritance) is a place with Him in heaven. We can accept this free gift by believing that Jesus is our Savior.

Jacob's Ladder

Genesis 28:12–13

MEMORY VERSE:
Surely goodness and mercy shall follow me all the days of my life; and I will dwell in the house of the LORD forever.

—*Psalm 23:6*

28 ... ¹²Then he dreamed, and behold, a ladder was set up on the earth, and its top reached to heaven; and there the angels of God were ascending and descending on it.

¹³And behold, the LORD stood above it and said: "I am the LORD God of Abraham your father and the God of Isaac; the land on which you lie I will give to you and your descendants.

DISCOVER:
What if you dreamed of a ladder to heaven like Jacob did and found out your dream was real? Would you be afraid?

UNDERSTAND:
Jacob was afraid at first. Then he made a vow to serve God.

LIVE IT OUT:
God has said He will never leave or forsake those who serve Him. To serve God you must believe and trust in Him.

JOSEPH SOLD BY HIS BROTHERS

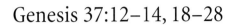

Genesis 37:12–14, 18–28

MEMORY VERSE:
Now Israel loved Joseph more than all his children, because he was the son of his old age. Also he made him a tunic of many colors.

—Genesis 37:3

37...¹²Then his brothers went to feed their father's flock in Shechem. ¹³And Israel said to Joseph, "Are not your brothers feeding the flock in Shechem? Come, I will send you to them."

So he said to him, "Here I am."

¹⁴Then he said to him [*Joseph*], "Please go and see if it is well with your brothers and well with the flocks, and bring back word to me." So he sent him out of the Valley of Hebron, and he went to Shechem....

¹⁸Now when they saw him afar off, even before he came near them, they conspired against him to kill him. ¹⁹Then they said to one another, "Look, this dreamer is coming! ²⁰Come therefore, let us now kill

him and cast him into some pit; and we shall say, 'Some wild beast has devoured him.' We shall see what will become of his dreams!"

21But Reuben heard it, and he delivered him out of their hands, and said, "Let us not kill him." 22And Reuben said to them, "Shed no blood, but cast him into this pit which is in the wilderness, and do not lay a hand on him"—that he might deliver him out of their hands, and bring him back to his father.

²³So it came to pass, when Joseph had come to his brothers, that they stripped Joseph of his tunic, the tunic of many colors that was on him. ²⁴Then they took him and cast him into a pit. And the pit was empty; there was no water in it.

²⁵And they sat down to eat a meal. Then they lifted their eyes and looked, and there was a company of Ishmaelites, coming from Gilead with their camels, bearing spices, balm, and myrrh, on their way to carry them down to Egypt. ²⁶So Judah said to his brothers, "What

profit is there if we kill our brother and conceal his blood? ²⁷Come and let us sell him to the Ishmaelites, and let not our hand be upon him, for he is our brother and our flesh." And his brothers listened. ²⁸Then Midianite traders passed by; so the brothers pulled Joseph up and lifted him out of the pit, and sold him to the Ishmaelites for twenty shekels of silver. And they took Joseph to Egypt.

DISCOVER:

Joseph's brothers called him a "dreamer." They were jealous of Joseph and wanted to get rid of him, so they threw him into a deep hole to die. What happened next?

UNDERSTAND:

God had plans for Joseph, and He did not let Joseph die. Joseph's brothers sold him to the Ishmaelites for twenty shekels of silver, which is very little money.

LIVE IT OUT:

God has plans for us, too, but we don't know what those plans are. We should ask God to help us to do His will and live according to His plan.

JOSEPH SENT TO PRISON

Genesis 39:1–5, 7–9, 11–12, 16–18, 20–21, 23

MEMORY VERSE:
But you, O man of God, flee these things and pursue
righteousness, godliness, faith, love, patience, gentleness.

—I Timothy 6:11

39 Now Joseph had been taken down to Egypt. And Potiphar, an officer of Pharaoh, captain of the guard, an Egyptian, bought him from the Ishmaelites who had taken him down there. ²The LORD was with Joseph, and he was a successful man; and he was in the house of his master the Egyptian. ³And his master saw that the LORD was with him and that the LORD made all he did to prosper in his hand. ⁴So Joseph found favor in his sight, and served him. Then he made him overseer of his house, and all that he had he put under his authority. ⁵So it was, from the time that he had made him overseer of his house and all that he had, that the LORD blessed the Egyptian's house for Joseph's sake; and the blessing of the LORD was on all that he had in the house and in the field. . . .

⁷And it came to pass after these things that his master's wife cast longing eyes on Joseph, and she said, "Lie with me."

⁸But he refused and said to his master's wife, "Look, my master does not know what is with me in the house, and he has committed all that he has to my hand. ⁹There is no one greater in this house than I,

nor has he kept back anything from me but you, because you are his wife. How then can I do this great wickedness, and sin against God?"...

¹¹But it happened about this time, when Joseph went into the house to do his work, and none of the men of the house was inside, ¹²that she caught him by his garment, saying, "Lie with me." But he left his garment in her hand, and fled and ran outside....

¹⁶So she kept his garment with her until his master came home. ¹⁷Then she spoke to him with words like these, saying, "The Hebrew servant whom you brought to us came in to me to mock me; ¹⁸so it happened, as I lifted my voice and cried out, that he left his garment with me and fled outside."...

²⁰Then Joseph's master took him and put him into the prison, a place where the king's prisoners were confined. And he was there in the prison. ²¹But the LORD was with Joseph and showed him mercy,

and He gave him favor in the sight of the keeper of the prison.... ²³The keeper of the prison did not look into anything that was under Joseph's authority, because the Lord was with him; and whatever he did, the Lord made it prosper.

DISCOVER
Joseph always did his best. Whatever Joseph did, the Lord made it prosper. Whose wife tricked Joseph? Who sent Joseph to prison?

UNDERSTAND:
When Joseph was in prison, he continued to do his best. The Lord was with Joseph and showed him mercy.

LIVE IT OUT:
The Lord is our source of mercy. The Lord will reward us, but like Joseph we must be patient and always do our best.

JOSEPH INTERPRETS PHARAOH'S DREAMS

Genesis 41:16–27

MEMORY VERSE:
Having then gifts differing according to the grace that is
given to us, let us use them ....

—*Romans 12:6*

41 *Pharaoh had two dreams that he did not understand. The dreams troubled him so much that he sent for all the magicians and wise men of Egypt. And Pharaoh told them his dreams, but no one could interpret the dreams for Pharaoh. Then the chief butler spoke to Pharaoh and told him that while he was in prison, Joseph, a young Hebrew man, had correctly interpreted his dream and the dream of the chief baker. Pharaoh sent for Joseph and asked Joseph to tell him what his dreams meant.*

16So Joseph answered Pharaoh, saying, "It is not in me; God will give Pharaoh an answer of peace."

17Then Pharaoh said to Joseph: "Behold, in my dream I stood on the bank of the river. 18Suddenly seven cows came up out of the river, fine looking and fat; and they fed in the meadow. 19Then behold, seven other cows came up after them, poor and very ugly and gaunt, such ugliness as I have never seen in all the land of Egypt. 20And the gaunt and ugly cows ate up the first seven, the fat cows. 21When they had eaten them up, no one would have known that they had eaten them, for they were

just as ugly as at the beginning. So I awoke. ²²Also I saw in my dream, and suddenly seven heads came up on one stalk, full and good. ²³Then behold, seven heads, withered, thin, and blighted by the east wind, sprang up after them. ²⁴And the thin heads devoured the seven good heads. So I told this to the magicians, but there was no one who could explain it to me."

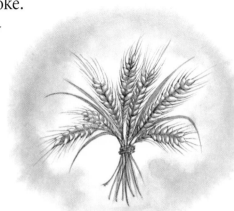

   ²⁵Then Joseph said to Pharaoh, "The dreams of Pharaoh are one; God has shown Pharaoh what He is about to do: ²⁶The seven good cows are seven years, and the seven good heads are seven years; the dreams are one. ²⁷And the seven thin and ugly cows which came up after them are seven years, and the seven empty heads blighted by the east wind are seven years of famine." . . .

Pharaoh knew the Spirit of God was in Joseph, so Pharaoh made Joseph ruler over all the land of Egypt. And Pharaoh called Joseph's name Zaphnath-Paaneah. And he gave him as a wife Asenath, the daughter of Poti-Pherah priest of On.

Everything Joseph said came to pass. But the people of Egypt had food during the famine because Joseph had stored food during the seven years of abundant harvest.

DISCOVER:
Pharaoh had great power. Why did Pharaoh send for Joseph? What did Joseph say?

UNDERSTAND:
God gave Joseph the ability to understand the meaning of dreams. It was because Joseph was able to understand Pharaoh's dreams that there was food during the famine and the people of Egypt did not starve.

LIVE IT OUT:
God gives everyone different abilities. We should respect another's gifts or talents, and use our own talents to glorify God.

Joseph Repays Brothers with Kindness

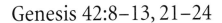

Genesis 42:8–13, 21–24

MEMORY VERSE:
"And you shall know the truth, and the truth shall make you free."

—John 8:32

42...⁸So Joseph recognized his brothers, but they did not recognize him. ⁹Then Joseph remembered the dreams which he had dreamed about them, and said to them, "You are spies! You have come to see the nakedness of the land!"

¹⁰And they said to him, "No, my lord, but your servants have come to buy food. ¹¹We are all one man's sons; we are honest men; your servants are not spies."

¹²But he said to them, "No, but you have come to see the nakedness of the land."

¹³And they said, "Your servants are twelve brothers, the sons of one man in the land of Canaan; and in fact, the youngest is with our father today, and one is no more." . . .

Joseph tested his brothers by throwing them in prison and sending one home to Canaan for the youngest brother. On the third day Joseph told them if they were honest men, they could go back home with the grain for their families and leave only one brother in prison. If they returned to Egypt with their youngest brother, the life of the brother left in prison would be spared. The brothers agreed.

. . . [21]Then they said to one another, "We are truly guilty concerning our brother, for we saw the anguish of his soul when he pleaded with us, and we would not hear; therefore this distress has come upon us."

²²And Reuben answered them, saying, "Did I not speak to you, saying, 'Do not sin against the boy'; and you would not listen? Therefore behold, his blood is now required of us." ²³But they did not know that Joseph understood them, for he spoke to them through an interpreter. ²⁴And he turned himself away from them and wept. Then he returned to them again, and talked with them. And he took Simeon from them and bound him before their eyes. . . .

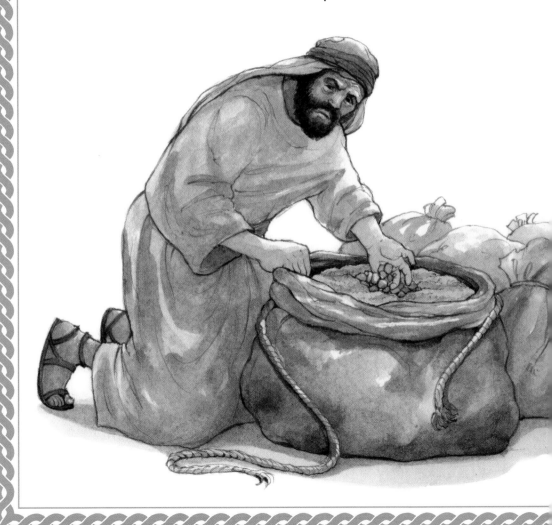

Then Joseph ordered that their sacks be filled with grain, that the money be restored to each brother's sack, and that they be given provisions for their journey. On the way home, one of the brothers opened his sack and saw that his money was in the sack along with the grain. When the brothers returned home, they discovered that all their sacks contained grain and money, and they were afraid that Joseph would think they had stolen the money. They told their father about meeting the ruler of all the land in Egypt and what had happened. But they still didn't know that the ruler was Joseph.

DISCOVER:
Why were Joseph's brothers in Egypt? Why did Joseph pretend he didn't know his brothers?

UNDERSTAND:
Joseph could have been vengeful to his brothers and refused them food. They and their families would have starved to death. But Joseph was forgiving, because he knew it was part of God's plan for him to come to Egypt. So Joseph never tried to "pay back" his brothers for the wrong they had done to him.

LIVE IT OUT:
When someone does something wrong to you, try to love that person instead of seeking revenge.

JOSEPH'S FAMILY MOVES TO EGYPT

Genesis 45:1–9, 13, 28

MEMORY VERSE:
And above all things have fervent love for one another, for
"love will cover a multitude of sins."

—1 Peter 4:8

45 Then Joseph could not restrain himself before all those who
stood by him, and he cried out, "Make everyone go out from me!" So
no one stood with him while Joseph made himself known to his
brothers. ²And he wept aloud, and the Egyptians and the house of
Pharaoh heard it.

³Then Joseph said to his brothers, "I am Joseph; does my father still
live?" But his brothers could not answer him, for they were dismayed in
his presence. ⁴And Joseph said to his brothers, "Please come near to me."
So they came near. Then he said: "I am Joseph your brother, whom you
sold into Egypt. ⁵But now, do not therefore be grieved or angry with
yourselves because you sold me here; for God sent me before you to
preserve life. ⁶For these two years the famine has been in the land, and
there are still five years in which there will be neither plowing nor
harvesting. ⁷And God sent me before you to preserve a posterity for
you in the earth, and to save your lives by a great deliverance. ⁸So now
it was not you who sent me here, but God; and He has made me a

father to Pharaoh, and lord of all his house, and a ruler throughout all the land of Egypt.

9"Hurry and go up to my father, and say to him, 'Thus says your son Joseph: "God has made me lord of all Egypt; come down to me, do not tarry. . . .

13So you shall tell my father of all my glory in Egypt, and of all that you have seen; and you shall hurry and bring my father down here." . . .

When Pharaoh heard that Joseph's brothers had come to Egypt, he was pleased. He told Joseph to have them return with their families and Pharaoh would give them the best land in Egypt.

Joseph gave his brothers more than they needed for their trip, and sent his father ten donkeys loaded with grain, bread, and food. And so the brothers left.

In Canaan they told their father that Joseph was alive and was ruler of all the land in Egypt. Jacob was so happy that his son was alive.

28 Then Israel *[Jacob]* said, "It is enough. Joseph my son is still alive. I will go and see him before I die." . . .

And so Joseph's family went to Egypt to live near him, and they were happy to be together again.

DISCOVER:
How did Joseph reveal himself to his brothers? What did Joseph tell his brothers to do?

UNDERSTAND:
Joseph loved his family. He wanted them to come live near him in Egypt.

LIVE IT OUT:
Sometimes we get mad at our brother or our sister. But love your family and forgive them when they do something that makes you unhappy.

Moses and the Burning Bush

Exodus 3:1–10

MEMORY VERSE:
"Then the LORD said to him, 'Take your sandals off your feet, for the place where you stand is holy ground.'"

—*Acts 7:33*

3Now Moses was tending the flock of Jethro his father-in-law, the priest of Midian. And he led the flock to the back of the desert, and came to Horeb, the mountain of God. ²And the Angel of the LORD appeared to him in a flame of fire from the midst of a bush. So he looked, and behold, the bush was burning with fire, but the bush was not consumed. ³Then Moses said, "I will now turn aside and see this great sight, why the bush does not burn."

⁴So when the LORD saw that he turned aside to look, God called to him from the midst of the bush and said, "Moses, Moses!"

And he said, "Here I am."

⁵Then He said, "Do not draw near this place. Take your sandals off your feet, for the place where you stand is holy ground." ⁶Moreover He said, "I am the God of your father—the God of Abraham, the God of Isaac, and the God of Jacob." And Moses hid his face, for he was afraid to look upon God.

⁷And the Lᴏʀᴅ said: "I have surely seen the oppression of My people who are in Egypt, and have heard their cry because of their taskmasters, for I know their sorrows. ⁸So I have come down to deliver them out of the hand of the Egyptians, and to bring them up from that land to a good and large land, to a land flowing with milk and honey,

to the place of the Canaanites and the Hittites and the Amorites and the Perizzites and the Hivites and the Jebusites. ⁹Now therefore, behold, the cry of the children of Israel has come to Me, and I have also seen the oppression with which the Egyptians oppress them. ¹⁰Come now, therefore, and I will send you to Pharaoh that you may bring My people, the children of Israel, out of Egypt."

DISCOVER:
Moses was taking care of his father-in-law's animals. What was the name of the mountain where Moses was tending the flock? Who spoke to Moses?

UNDERSTAND:
The angel of the Lord appeared to Moses in the fire of the burning bush. God called to Moses from the middle of the bush.

LIVE IT OUT:
Even though Moses was afraid when God spoke, Moses answered, "Here I am." We should always be willing to do God's work and say, "Here I am. Lead me."

GOD PARTS THE RED SEA

Exodus 14:5–7, 10–18, 21–22

MEMORY VERSE:
"You must not fear them, for the LORD your God Himself fights for you."

—Deuteronomy 3:22

14...⁵Now it was told the king of Egypt that the people had fled, and the heart of Pharaoh and his servants was turned against the people; and they said, "Why have we done this, that we have let Israel go from serving us?" ⁶So he made ready his chariot and took his people with him. ⁷Also, he took six hundred choice chariots, and all the chariots of Egypt with captains over every one of them....

¹⁰And when Pharaoh drew near, the children of Israel lifted their eyes, and behold, the Egyptians marched after them. So they were very afraid, and the children of Israel cried out to the LORD. ¹¹Then they said to Moses, "Because there were no graves in Egypt, have you taken us away to die in the wilderness? Why have you so dealt with us, to bring us up out of Egypt? ¹²Is this not the word that we told you in Egypt, saying, 'Let us alone that we may serve the Egyptians'? For it would have been better for us to serve the Egyptians than that we should die in the wilderness."

¹³And Moses said to the people, "Do not be afraid. Stand still, and see the salvation of the Lord, which He will accomplish for you today.

For the Egyptians whom you see today, you shall see again no more forever. ¹⁴The LORD will fight for you, and you shall hold your peace."

¹⁵And the LORD said to Moses, "Why do you cry to Me? Tell the children of Israel to go forward. ¹⁶But lift up your rod, and stretch out your hand over the sea and divide it. And the children of Israel shall go on dry ground through the midst of the sea. ¹⁷And I indeed will harden the hearts of the Egyptians, and they shall follow them. So I will gain honor over Pharaoh and over all his army, his chariots, and his horsemen. ¹⁸Then the Egyptians shall know that I am the LORD, when I have gained honor for Myself over Pharaoh, his chariots, and his horsemen."...

²¹Then Moses stretched out his hand over the sea; and the LORD caused the sea to go back by a strong east wind all that night, and made the sea into dry land, and the waters were divided. ²²So the children of Israel went into the midst of the sea on the dry ground, and the waters were a wall to them on their right hand and on their left.

DISCOVER:
The children of Israel complained to Moses. What did the Lord say to Moses? How did the children of Israel escape from the king of Egypt?

UNDERSTAND:
The children of Israel were not really all children, but people of many ages. Believers are children of the Lord, too, no matter how old we are.

LIVE IT OUT:
If you do what is right and pray for God's help, He will always fight for you.

THE WALLS OF JERICHO FALL

Joshua 6:1–7, 11, 14–17, 20

MEMORY VERSE:
By faith the walls of Jericho fell down after they were
encircled for seven days.

—Hebrews 11:30

6Now Jericho was securely shut up because of the children of Israel;
none went out, and none came in. 2And the LORD said to Joshua: "See! I
have given Jericho into your hand, its king, and the mighty men of valor.
3You shall march around the city, all you men of war; you shall go all
around the city once. This you shall do six days. 4And seven priests
shall bear seven trumpets of rams' horns before the ark. But the
seventh day you shall march around the city seven times, and the
priests shall blow the trumpets. 5It shall come to pass, when they make
a long blast with the ram's horn, and when you hear the sound of the
trumpet, that all the people shall shout with a great shout; then the
wall of the city will fall down flat. And the people shall go up every
man straight before him."

6Then Joshua the son of Nun called the priests and said to them,
"Take up the ark of the covenant, and let seven priests bear seven
trumpets of rams' horns before the ark of the LORD." 7And he said to
the people, "Proceed, and march around the city, and let him who is
armed advance before the ark of the LORD." . . .

¹¹So he had the ark of the LORD circle the city, going around it once. Then they came into the camp and lodged in the camp. . . .

¹⁴And the second day they marched around the city once and returned to the camp. So they did six days.

¹⁵But it came to pass on the seventh day that they rose early, about the dawning of the day, and marched around the city seven times in the same manner. On that day only they marched around the city seven times. ¹⁶And the seventh time it happened, when the priests blew the trumpets, that Joshua said to the people: "Shout, for the LORD

has given you the city! ¹⁷Now the city shall be doomed by the LORD to destruction, it and all who are in it. Only Rahab the harlot shall live, she and all who are with her in the house, because she hid the messengers that we sent."...

²⁰So the people shouted when the priests blew the trumpets. And it happened when the people heard the sound of the trumpet, and the people shouted with a great shout, that the wall fell down flat. Then the people went up into the city, every man straight before him, and they took the city.

DISCOVER:
What were the seven trumpets made of? What happened when the priests blew the trumpets and the people shouted?

UNDERSTAND:
The fall of the wall of Jericho is sometimes called a miracle, because it shows the power of God.

LIVE IT OUT:
We should always follow God's instructions exactly. We can do this by studying the Bible often and learning His instructions.

THE DAY THE SUN STOOD STILL

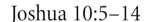

Joshua 10:5–14

10...⁵Therefore the five kings of the Amorites, the king of Jerusalem, the king of Hebron, the king of Jarmuth, the king of Lachish, and the king of Eglon, gathered together and went up, they and all their armies, and camped before Gibeon and made war against it.

⁶And the men of Gibeon sent to Joshua at the camp at Gilgal, saying, "Do not forsake your servants; come up to us quickly, save us and help us, for all the kings of the Amorites who dwell in the mountains have gathered together against us."

⁷So Joshua ascended from Gilgal, he and all the people of war with him, and all the mighty men of valor. ⁸And the LORD said to Joshua, "Do not fear them, for I have delivered them into your hand; not a man of them shall stand before you." ⁹Joshua therefore came upon them suddenly, having marched all night from Gilgal. ¹⁰So the LORD routed them before Israel, killed them with a great slaughter at Gibeon, chased them along the road that goes to Beth Horon, and struck them down as far as Azekah and Makkedah. ¹¹And it happened, as they fled before Israel and were on the descent of Beth Horon, that the LORD cast down

large hailstones from heaven on them as far as Azekah, and they died. There were more who died from the hailstones than the children of Israel killed with the sword.

¹²Then Joshua spoke to the LORD in the day when the LORD delivered up the Amorites before the children of Israel, and he said in the sight of Israel: "Sun, stand still over Gibeon; and Moon, in the Valley of Aijalon."

¹³So the sun stood still, and the moon stopped, till the people had revenge upon their enemies. Is this not written in the Book of Jasher?

So the sun stood still in the midst of heaven, and did not hasten to go down for about a whole day. [14]And there has been no day like that, before it or after it, that the LORD heeded the voice of a man; for the LORD fought for Israel.

DISCOVER:
How was it possible for Joshua to tell the sun to stand still?

UNDERSTAND:
The Lord told Joshua not to fear his enemies. The Lord would keep Joshua's people safe.

LIVE IT OUT:
Seek the Lord, and He will hear you and deliver you from all your fears.

Delilah Tricks Samson

Judges 16:4–10, 16–17, 19–22

MEMORY VERSE:
Let no one deceive you with empty words, for because of these things the wrath of God comes upon the sons of disobedience.

—*Ephesians 5:6*

16 ...⁴Afterward it happened that he loved a woman in the Valley of Sorek, whose name was Delilah. ⁵And the lords of the Philistines came up to her and said to her, "Entice him, and find out where his great strength lies, and by what means we may overpower him, that we may bind him to afflict him; and every one of us will give you eleven hundred pieces of silver."

⁶So Delilah said to Samson, "Please tell me where your great strength lies, and with what you may be bound to afflict you."

⁷And Samson said to her, "If they bind me with seven fresh bowstrings, not yet dried, then I shall become weak, and be like any other man."

⁸So the lords of the Philistines brought up to her seven fresh bowstrings, not yet dried, and she bound him with them. ⁹Now men were lying in wait, staying with her in the room. And she said to him, "The Philistines are upon you, Samson!" But he broke the bowstrings as a strand of yarn breaks when it touches fire. So the secret of his strength was not known.

¹⁰Then Delilah said to Samson, "Look, you have mocked me and told me lies. Now, please tell me what you may be bound with."...

¹⁶And it came to pass, when she pestered him daily with her words and pressed him, so that his soul was vexed to death, ¹⁷that he told her all his heart, and said to her, "No razor has ever come upon my head, for I have been a Nazirite to God from my mother's womb. If I am shaven, then my strength will leave me, and I shall become weak, and be like any other man."...

¹⁹Then she lulled him to sleep on her knees, and called for a man and had him shave off the seven locks of his head. Then she began to

torment him, and his strength left him. ²⁰And she said, "The Philistines are upon you, Samson!" So he awoke from his sleep, and said, "I will go out as before, at other times, and shake myself free!" But he did not know that the LORD had departed from him.

²¹Then the Philistines took him and put out his eyes, and brought him down to Gaza. They bound him with bronze fetters, and he became a grinder in the prison. ²²However, the hair of his head began to grow again after it had been shaven.

DISCOVER:

Do you think Delilah was a good person? Was Samson sometimes foolish? Why did Delilah trick Samson?

UNDERSTAND:

Delilah did not like Samson; she was greedy and wanted money. The Philistines hated Samson; they wanted to imprison one of God's strongest warriors. Together, they tricked Samson into telling his secret and losing the strength God had given him.

LIVE IT OUT:

People will sometimes try to deceive us. Pray for wisdom to make the right choices.

SAMSON: THE STRONGEST MAN

Judges 16:23–30

MEMORY VERSE:
"For You have armed me with strength for the battle; You
have subdued under me those who rose against me."

—*2 Samuel 22:40*

16... ²³Now the lords of the Philistines gathered together to offer a great sacrifice to Dagon their god, and to rejoice. And they said: "Our god has delivered into our hands Samson our enemy!"

²⁴When the people saw him, they praised their god; for they said: "Our god has delivered into our hands our enemy, the destroyer of our land, and the one who multiplied our dead."

²⁵So it happened, when their hearts were merry, that they said, "Call for Samson, that he may perform for us." So they called for Samson from the prison, and he performed for them. And they stationed him between the pillars. ²⁶Then Samson said to the lad who held him by the hand, "Let me feel the pillars which support the temple, so that I can lean on them." ²⁷Now the temple was full of men and women. All the lords of the Philistines were there—about three thousand men and women on the roof watching while Samson performed.

²⁸Then Samson called to the LORD, saying, "O Lord GOD, remember me, I pray! Strengthen me, I pray, just this once, O God, that I may with one blow take vengeance on the Philistines for my two eyes!" ²⁹And

Samson took hold of the two middle pillars which supported the temple, and he braced himself against them, one on his right and the other on his left. [30]Then Samson said, "Let me die with the Philistines!" And he pushed with all his might, and the temple fell on the lords and all the people who were in it. So the dead that he killed at his death were more than he had killed in his life.

DISCOVER:
Why did the lords of the Philistines want to offer a great sacrifice to Dagon, a false god?

UNDERSTAND:
Samson was a fierce warrior. He had fought the Philistines, killing many and destroying their crops. The Philistines captured Samson and put him in prison. They were very cruel to Samson and blinded him.

LIVE IT OUT:
Samson prayed for the Lord to remember him and give him strength, and the Lord did. Our strength also comes from the Lord.

RUTH AND BOAZ

Ruth 2:1–3, 12

MEMORY VERSE:
But the fruit of the Spirit is love, joy, peace, longsuffering,
kindness, goodness, faithfulness, gentleness, self-control.
Against such there is no law.

—Galatians 5:22

2There was a relative of Naomi's husband, a man of great wealth, of the family of Elimelech. His name was Boaz. 2So Ruth the Moabitess said to Naomi, "Please let me go to the field, and glean heads of grain after him in whose sight I may find favor."

And she said to her, "Go, my daughter."

3Then she left, and went and gleaned in the field after the reapers.

And she happened to come to the part of the field belonging to Boaz, who was of the family of Elimelech. . . .

Boaz noticed Ruth in the field and asked a servant who she was. Boaz had heard about everything Ruth had done for her mother-in-law, Naomi. He was impressed by Ruth's loyalty. Boaz offered Ruth water to drink and asked her to stay in his field to work. Boaz loved Ruth and wanted to protect her. Boaz was very kind to Ruth. He said. . .

". . . 12The LORD repay your work, and a full reward be given you by the LORD God of Israel, under whose wings you have come for refuge." . . .

Boaz and Ruth married, and their son was named Obed. He is the father of Jesse, who is the father of David. And it was David who fought Goliath.

DISCOVER:
Where did Ruth go to gather crops? Who did she meet there and marry?

UNDERSTAND:
It was against the law for the landowners to glean their fields and orchards. Anything missed by the reapers and gatherers, was left for the poor to pick. Boaz was a kind and just man who obeyed the law.

LIVE IT OUT:
God wants us to follow in His footsteps and be kind to others, as Boaz was kind to Ruth.

HANNAH GIVES SAMUEL TO THE LORD

1 Samuel 1:19–28

MEMORY VERSE:
And Hannah prayed and said: . . . "No one is holy like the
LORD, for there is none besides You, nor is there any rock
like our God."

—*1 Samuel 2:1, 2*

1...¹⁹Then they rose early in the morning and worshiped before the
LORD, and returned and came to their house at Ramah. And Elkanah
knew Hannah his wife, and the LORD remembered her. ²⁰So it came
to pass in the process of time that Hannah conceived and bore a son,
and called his name Samuel, saying, "Because I have asked for him
from the LORD."

²¹Now the man Elkanah and all his house went up to offer to the
LORD the yearly sacrifice and his vow. ²²But Hannah did not go up, for
she said to her husband, "Not until the child is weaned; then I will take
him, that he may appear before the LORD and remain there forever."

²³So Elkanah her husband said to her, "Do what seems best to you;
wait until you have weaned him. Only let the LORD establish His word."
Then the woman stayed and nursed her son until she had weaned him.

²⁴Now when she had weaned him, she took him up with her, with three bulls, one ephah of flour, and a skin of wine, and brought him to the house of the LORD in Shiloh. And the child was young. ²⁵Then they slaughtered a bull, and brought the child to Eli. ²⁶And she said, "O my lord! As your soul lives, my lord, I am the woman who stood by you here, praying to the LORD. ²⁷For this child I prayed, and the LORD has

granted me my petition which I asked of Him. [28]Therefore I also have lent him to the Lord; as long as he lives he shall be lent to the Lord." So they worshiped the Lord there.

DISCOVER:
What did Hannah ask God for? What did Hannah bring with her to Shiloh?

UNDERSTAND:
God granted Hannah's request for a child, which made her very happy, and she praised God and kept her promise.

LIVE IT OUT:
It easy to make promises but sometimes harder to keep them. Try to keep your promises to God.

SAMUEL ANSWERS THE LORD

1 Samuel 3:1–13, 17–19

MEMORY VERSE:
"Call to Me, and I will answer you, and show you great
and mighty things, which you do not know."

—*Jeremiah 33:3*

3 Now the boy Samuel ministered to the LORD before Eli. And the word of the LORD was rare in those days; there was no widespread revelation. ²And it came to pass at that time, while Eli was lying down in his place, and when his eyes had begun to grow so dim that he could not see, ³and before the lamp of God went out in the tabernacle of the LORD where the ark of God was, and while Samuel was lying down, ⁴that the LORD called Samuel. And he answered, "Here I am!" ⁵So he ran to Eli and said, "Here I am, for you called me."

And he said, "I did not call; lie down again." And he went and lay down.

⁶Then the LORD called yet again, "Samuel!"

So Samuel arose and went to Eli, and said, "Here I am, for you called me." He answered, "I did not call, my son; lie down again." ⁷(Now Samuel did not yet know the LORD, nor was the word of the LORD yet revealed to him.)

8And the LORD called Samuel again the third time. So he arose and went to Eli, and said, "Here I am, for you did call me."

Then Eli perceived that the LORD had called the boy. 9Therefore Eli said to Samuel, "Go, lie down; and it shall be, if He calls you, that you must say, 'Speak, LORD, for Your servant hears.'" So Samuel went and lay down in his place.

10Now the LORD came and stood and called as at other times, "Samuel! Samuel!"

And Samuel answered, "Speak, for Your servant hears."

11Then the LORD said to Samuel: "Behold, I will do something in Israel at which both ears of everyone who hears it will tingle. 12In that day I will perform against Eli all that I have spoken concerning his house, from beginning to end. 13For I have told him that I will judge his house forever for the iniquity which he knows, because his sons made themselves vile, and he did not restrain them."...

17And he [Eli] said, "What is the word that the LORD spoke to you? Please do not hide it from me. God do so to you, and more also, if you hide anything from me of all the things that He said to you." 18Then Samuel told him everything, and hid nothing from him. And he said, "It is the LORD. Let Him do what seems good to Him."

19So Samuel grew, and the LORD was with him and let none of his words fall to the ground.

DISCOVER:

Who did Samuel think called him? Had the Lord's word been revealed to Samuel at this time?

UNDERSTAND:

Samuel had not been told about the Lord. He didn't know who had called him, but Eli did. Samuel became a servant of the Lord. This was the first of many times the Lord spoke to Samuel.

LIVE IT OUT:

The Lord is always with His servants. Are you a servant of the Lord?

SAUL REBELS AGAINST GOD

1 Samuel 15:10–23

MEMORY VERSE:
Let him turn away from evil and do good; let him seek
peace and pursue it.

—1 Peter 3:11

15...¹⁰Now the word of the LORD came to Samuel, saying, ¹¹"I greatly regret that I have set up Saul as king, for he has turned back from following Me, and has not performed My commandments." And it grieved Samuel, and he cried out to the LORD all night. ¹²So when Samuel rose early in the morning to meet Saul, it was told Samuel, saying, "Saul went to Carmel, and indeed, he set up a monument for himself; and he has gone on around, passed by, and gone down to Gilgal." ¹³Then Samuel went to Saul, and Saul said to him, "Blessed are you of the LORD! I have performed the commandment of the LORD."

¹⁴But Samuel said, "What then is this bleating of the sheep in my ears, and the lowing of the oxen which I hear?"

¹⁵And Saul said, "They have brought them from the Amalekites; for the people spared the best of the sheep and the oxen, to sacrifice to the LORD your God; and the rest we have utterly destroyed."

¹⁶Then Samuel said to Saul, "Be quiet! And I will tell you what the LORD said to me last night."

And he said to him, "Speak on."

¹⁷So Samuel said, "When you were little in your own eyes, were you not head of the tribes of Israel? And did not the LORD anoint you king over Israel? ¹⁸Now the LORD sent you on a mission, and said, 'Go, and utterly destroy the sinners, the Amalekites, and fight against them until they are consumed.' ¹⁹Why then did you not obey the voice of the LORD? Why did you swoop down on the spoil, and do evil in the sight of the LORD?"

²⁰And Saul said to Samuel, "But I have obeyed the voice of the LORD, and gone on the mission on which the LORD sent me, and brought back Agag king of Amalek; I have utterly destroyed the Amalekites. ²¹But the people took of the plunder, sheep and oxen, the best of the things which should have been utterly destroyed, to sacrifice to the LORD your God in Gilgal."

²²So Samuel said: "Has the LORD as great delight in burnt offerings and sacrifices, as in obeying the voice of the LORD? Behold, to obey is better than sacrifice, and to heed than the fat of rams. ²³For rebellion is as the sin of witchcraft, and stubbornness is as iniquity and idolatry. Because you have rejected the word of the LORD, He also has rejected you from being king."

DISCOVER:

Saul turned away from the Lord. Why did Saul reject the Word of the Lord? Do you think it was because Saul liked to do things his way?

UNDERSTAND:

The Lord was not pleased with Saul, for Saul had been stubborn and had not followed the Lord's instructions.

LIVE IT OUT:

Be careful not to be stubborn and rebellious like Saul, who did things his way. The Lord's way is always the right way.

DAVID PLAYS THE HARP FOR SAUL

1 Samuel 16:13b, 14–23

16...¹³And the Spirit of the LORD came upon David....

¹⁴But the Spirit of the LORD departed from Saul, and a distressing spirit from the LORD troubled him.

¹⁵And Saul's servants said to him, "Surely, a distressing spirit from God is troubling you.¹⁶Let our master now command your servants, who are before you, to seek out a man who is a skillful player on the harp. And it shall be that he will play it with his hand when the distressing spirit from God is upon you, and you shall be well."

¹⁷So Saul said to his servants, "Provide me now a man who can play well, and bring him to me."

¹⁸Then one of the servants answered and said, "Look, I have seen a son of Jesse the Bethlehemite, who is skillful in playing, a mighty man of valor, a man of war, prudent in speech, and a handsome person; and the LORD is with him."

¹⁹Therefore Saul sent messengers to Jesse, and said, "Send me your

son David, who is with the sheep." 20And Jesse took a donkey loaded with bread, a skin of wine, and a young goat, and sent them by his son David to Saul. 21So David came to Saul and stood before him. And he loved him greatly, and he became his armorbearer. 22Then Saul sent to Jesse, saying, "Please let David stand before me, for he has found favor in my sight."

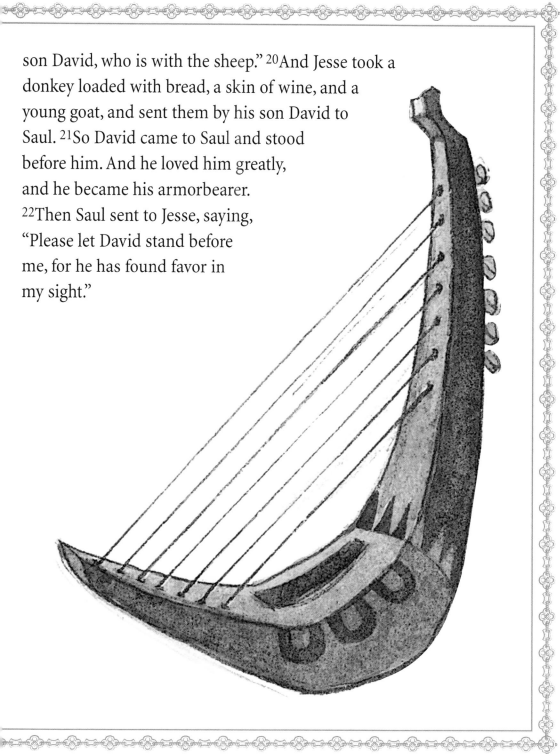

²³And so it was, whenever the spirit from God was upon Saul, that David would take a harp and play it with his hand. Then Saul would become refreshed and well, and the distressing spirit would depart from him.

DISCOVER:

Why did Saul send for David? What did David do to soothe Saul?

UNDERSTAND:

An armorbearer is a person who carries the fighting equipment of a warrior.

LIVE IT OUT:

David did not complain. He was pleased to obey the Lord. Do you cheerfully do all you can to obey the Lord?

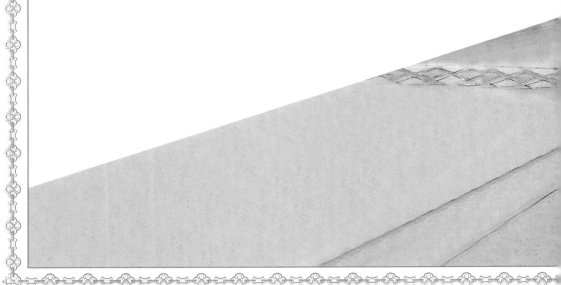

LITTLE DAVID SLAYS A GIANT

1 Samuel 17:3–9, 40, 43, 45, 49–50

MEMORY VERSE:
The LORD is good, a stronghold in the day of trouble;
and He knows those who trust in Him.

—Nahum 1:7

17...³The Philistines stood on a mountain on one side, and Israel stood on a mountain on the other side, with a valley between them.

⁴And a champion went out from the camp of the Philistines, named Goliath, from Gath, whose height was six cubits and a span. ⁵He had a bronze helmet on his head, and he was armed with a coat of mail, and the weight of the coat was five thousand shekels of bronze. ⁶And he had bronze armor on his legs and a bronze javelin between his shoulders. ⁷Now the staff of his spear was like a weaver's beam, and his iron spearhead weighed six hundred shekels; and a shield-bearer went before him. ⁸Then he stood and cried out to the armies of Israel, and said to them, "Why have you come out to line up for battle? Am I not a Philistine, and you the servants of Saul? Choose a man for yourselves, and let him come down to me. ⁹If he is able to fight with me and kill me, then we will be your servants. But if I prevail against him and kill him, then you shall be our servants and serve us."...

David's father sent David to the army camp to take food and check on his brothers. When Goliath again challenged the men of Israel, the men were afraid. But David wanted to fight Goliath. David convinced Saul that he was a brave warrior and that God would protect him.

⁴⁰Then he *[David]* took his staff in his hand; and he chose for himself five smooth stones from the brook, and put them in a shepherd's bag, in a pouch which he had, and his sling was in his hand. And he drew near to the Philistine. . . .

⁴³So the Philistine said to David, "Am I a dog, that you come to me with sticks?" And the Philistine cursed David by his gods. . . .

⁴⁵Then David said to the Philistine, "You come to me with a sword, with a spear, and with a javelin. But I come to you in the name of the LORD of hosts, the God of the armies of Israel, whom you have defied. . . ."

⁴⁹Then David put his hand in his bag and took out a stone; and he slung it and struck the Philistine in his forehead, so that the stone sank into his forehead, and he fell on his face to the earth. ⁵⁰So David prevailed over the Philistine with a sling and a stone, and struck the Philistine and killed him. But there was no sword in the hand of David.

DISCOVER:
Goliath thought he was a "superman." He was nine feet tall and his armor weighed 150 to 330 pounds.

UNDERSTAND:
David is noted in the Bible as being a man after God's own heart. Did David win because he fought in the name of the Lord?

LIVE IT OUT:
Reject evil and try to please God in everything you do.

DAVID SPARES SAUL'S LIFE

1 Samuel 24: 4, 8–13, 16–17, 19

MEMORY VERSE:
Do not be overcome by evil, but overcome evil with good.

—*Romans 12:21*

24 When Saul learned that David and his men were in the *Wilderness of En Gedi, Saul took three thousand men from Israel and went to find David and his men on the Rocks of the Wild Goats. By the road was a cave, and Saul went in to attend to his needs. Saul did not know that David and his men were staying deep inside the cave.*

⁴Then the men of David said to him, "This is the day of which the Lord said to you, 'Behold, I will deliver your enemy into your hand, that you may do to him as it seems good to you.'" And David arose and secretly cut off a corner of Saul's robe. . . .

Afterward, David felt bad for cutting Saul's robe. He didn't allow his servants to rise against Saul. And Saul, not knowing what had happened, got up from the cave and went on his way.

⁸David also arose afterward, went out of the cave, and called out to Saul, saying, "My lord the king!" And when Saul looked behind him, David stooped with his face to the earth, and bowed down. ⁹And David said to Saul: "Why do you listen to the words of men who say, 'Indeed David seeks your harm'? ¹⁰Look, this day your eyes have seen that the Lord delivered you today into my hand in the cave, and someone urged me to kill you. But my eye spared you, and I said, 'I will not stretch out my hand against my lord, for he is the Lord's anointed.' ¹¹Moreover, my father, see! Yes, see the corner of your robe in my hand! For in that I cut off the corner of your robe, and did not kill you, know and see that there is neither evil nor rebellion in my hand, and I have not sinned against you. Yet you hunt my life to take it. ¹²Let the Lord judge between you and me, and let the Lord avenge me on you. But my hand shall not be against you. ¹³As the proverb of the ancients says, 'Wickedness proceeds from the wicked.' But my hand shall not be against you. . . ."

16So it was, when David had finished speaking these words to Saul, that Saul said, "Is this your voice, my son David?" And Saul lifted up his voice and wept. 17Then he said to David: "You are more righteous than I; for you have rewarded me with good, whereas I have rewarded you with evil. . . .

19"For if a man finds his enemy, will he let him get away safely? Therefore may the LORD reward you with good for what you have done to me this day."

DISCOVER:
What did Saul say to David about a man finding his enemy? Who did God reward that day?

UNDERSTAND:
David could have harmed Saul. He was close enough, but he chose to do good. Rewarding evil with good is not easy.

LIVE IT OUT:
We should always try to answer evil deeds with good deeds.

Solomon's Wise Judgment

1 Kings 3:16–28

MEMORY VERSE:
And God gave Solomon wisdom and exceedingly great understanding, and largeness of heart like the sand on the seashore.

—Psalm 34:4

3... 16Now two women who were harlots came to the king, and stood before him. 17And one woman said, "O my lord, this woman and I dwell in the same house; and I gave birth while she was in the house. 18Then it happened, the third day after I had given birth, that this woman also gave birth. And we were together; no one was with us in the house, except the two of us in the house. 19And this woman's son died in the night, because she lay on him. 20So she arose in the middle of the night and took my son from my side, while your maidservant slept, and laid him in her bosom, and laid her dead child in my bosom. 21And when I rose in the morning to nurse my son, there he was, dead. But when I had examined him in the morning, indeed, he was not my son whom I had borne."

22Then the other woman said, "No! But the living one is my son, and the dead one is your son."

And the first woman said, "No! But the dead one is your son, and the living one is my son."

Thus they spoke before the king.

23And the king said, "The one says, 'This is my son, who lives, and your son is the dead one'; and the other says, 'No! But your son is the dead one, and my son is the living one.'" 24Then the king said, "Bring me a sword." So they brought a sword before the king. 25And the king said, "Divide the living child in two, and give half to one, and half to the other."

26Then the woman whose son was living spoke to the king, for she yearned with compassion for her son; and she said, "O my lord, give her the living child, and by no means kill him!"

But the other said, "Let him be neither mine nor yours, but divide him."

27So the king answered and said, "Give the first woman the living child, and by no means kill him; she is his mother."

28And all Israel heard of the judgment which the king had rendered; and they feared the king, for they saw that the wisdom of God was in him to administer justice.

DISCOVER:

What did Solomon say to the women to figure out who the child's mother was?

UNDERSTAND:

Solomon knew that the true mother would not allow her child to be killed, so he tested the two women.

LIVE IT OUT:

Solomon was known for his great wisdom. God gives us wisdom, too, when we read and study His Word. We must try to recognize and use the wisdom he gives us.

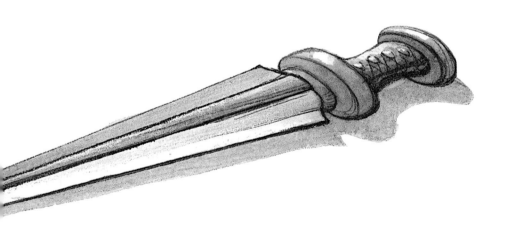

Elijah Helps a Widow

1 Kings 17:7–14, 21–24

MEMORY VERSE:
For the word of the LORD is right, and all His work is done in truth.

—*Psalm 33:4*

17...⁷And it happened after a while that the brook dried up, because there had been no rain in the land.

⁸Then the word of the LORD came to him, saying, ⁹"Arise, go to Zarephath, which belongs to Sidon, and dwell there. See, I have commanded a widow there to provide for you." ¹⁰So he arose and went to Zarephath. And when he came to the gate of the city, indeed a widow was there gathering sticks. And he called to her and said, "Please bring me a little water in a cup, that I may drink." ¹¹And as she

was going to get it, he called to her and said, "Please bring me a morsel of bread in your hand."

12So she said, "As the LORD your God lives, I do not have bread, only a handful of flour in a bin, and a little oil in a jar; and see, I am gathering a couple of sticks that I may go in and prepare it for myself and my son, that we may eat it, and die."

¹³And Elijah said to her, "Do not fear; go and do as you have said, but make me a small cake from it first, and bring it to me; and

afterward make some for yourself and your son. ¹⁴For thus says the LORD God of Israel: 'The bin of flour shall not be used up, nor shall the jar of oil run dry, until the day the LORD sends rain on the earth.'" . . .

What Elijah said was true, and they all ate for many days. Then the widow's son became very ill. The widow thought Elijah had made her son sick because of her sin.

²¹And he [*Elijah*] stretched himself out on the child three times, and cried out to the LORD and said, "O LORD my God, I pray, let this child's soul come back to him." ²²Then the LORD heard the voice of Elijah; and the soul of the child came back to him, and he revived.

²³And Elijah took the child and brought him down from the upper room into the house, and gave him to his mother. And Elijah said, "See, your son lives!"

²⁴Then the woman said to Elijah, "Now by this I know that you are a man of God, and that the word of the LORD in your mouth is the truth."

DISCOVER:
What did the Lord tell Elijah to do? Did Elijah do it?

UNDERSTAND:
The widow didn't know Elijah, but she believed he spoke the truth. Because she fed Elijah, she never ran out of oil and flour, and Elijah was there to save her son.

LIVE IT OUT:
When we are following God's will, others will see that we speak the truth.

Elijah Convinces Baal's Prophets

1 Kings 18:25–33, 37–39

MEMORY VERSE:
"You shall have no other gods before Me."

—Exodus 20:3

18… 25Now Elijah said to the prophets of Baal, "Choose one bull for yourselves and prepare it first, for you are many; and call on the name of your god, but put no fire under it."

26So they took the bull which was given them, and they prepared it, and called on the name of Baal from morning even till noon, saying, "O Baal, hear us!" But there was no voice; no one answered. Then they leaped about the altar which they had made.

27And so it was, at noon, that Elijah mocked them and said, "Cry aloud, for he is a god; either he is meditating, or he is busy, or he is on a journey, or perhaps he is sleeping and must be awakened." 28So they cried aloud, and cut themselves, as was their custom, with knives and lances, until the blood gushed out on them. 29And when midday was past, they prophesied until the time of the offering of the evening sacrifice. But there was no voice; no one answered, no one paid attention.

30Then Elijah said to all the people, "Come near to me." So all the people came near to him. And he repaired the altar of the Lord that was broken down. 31And Elijah took twelve stones, according to the number of the tribes of the sons of Jacob, to whom the word of the LORD had come, saying, "Israel shall be your name." 32Then with the stones he built an altar in the name of the LORD; and he made a trench around the altar large enough to hold two seahs of seed. 33And he put the wood in order, cut the bull in pieces, and laid it on the wood, and said, "Fill four waterpots with water, and pour it on the burnt sacrifice and on the wood."...

They did this three times, until water ran around the altar. Then Elijah filled the trench with water. And he said...

³⁷"Hear me, O LORD, hear me, that this people may know that You are the LORD God, and that You have turned their hearts back to You again."

³⁸Then the fire of the LORD fell and consumed the burnt sacrifice, and the wood and the stones and the dust, and it licked up the water that was in the trench. ³⁹Now when all the people saw it, they fell on their faces; and they said, "The LORD, He is God! The LORD, He is God!"

DISCOVER:
What was the meaning of the twelve stones Elijah took? How did the Lord convince the prophets of Baal that He was God?

UNDERSTAND:
The prophets of Baal prayed to a false god, and so their god was powerless to help them even light a fire.

LIVE IT OUT:
There is only one true God. We should praise only Him, and not be misled by false gods and material things.

Elijah Rides a Chariot of Fire

2 Kings 2:1–11

MEMORY VERSE:
That the God of our Lord Jesus Christ, the Father of glory, may give to you the spirit of wisdom and revelation in the knowledge of Him. . . .

—Ephesians 1:17

2And it came to pass, when the Lord was about to take up Elijah into heaven by a whirlwind, that Elijah went with Elisha from Gilgal. ²Then Elijah said to Elisha, "Stay here, please, for the Lord has sent me on to Bethel."

But Elisha said, "As the Lord lives, and as your soul lives, I will not leave you!" So they went down to Bethel.

³Now the sons of the prophets who were at Bethel came out to Elisha, and said to him, "Do you know that the Lord will take away your master from over you today?"

And he said, "Yes, I know; keep silent!"

⁴Then Elijah said to him, "Elisha, stay here, please, for the Lord has sent me on to Jericho."

But he said, "As the Lord lives, and as your soul lives, I will not leave you!" So they came to Jericho.

⁵Now the sons of the prophets who were at Jericho came to Elisha and said to him, "Do you know that the Lord will take away your master from over you today?"

So he answered, "Yes, I know; keep silent!"

⁶Then Elijah said to him, "Stay here, please, for the LORD has sent me on to the Jordan."

But he said, "As the LORD lives, and as your soul lives, I will not leave you!" So the two of them went on. ⁷And fifty men of the sons of the prophets went and stood facing them at a distance, while the two of them stood by the Jordan. ⁸Now Elijah took his mantle, rolled it up, and struck the water; and it was divided this way and that, so that the two of them crossed over on dry ground.

⁹And so it was, when they had crossed over, that Elijah said to Elisha, "Ask! What may I do for you, before I am taken away from you?"

Elisha said, "Please let a double portion of your spirit be upon me."

¹⁰So he said, "You have asked a hard thing. Nevertheless, if you see me when I am taken from you, it shall be so for you; but if not, it shall not be so." ¹¹Then it happened, as they continued on and talked, that suddenly a chariot of fire appeared with horses of fire, and separated the two of them; and Elijah went up by a whirlwind into heaven.

DISCOVER:
What did Elisha ask Elijah for before Elijah was taken up to heaven? How did Elijah get to heaven?

UNDERSTAND:
Elisha was loyal to Elijah and stayed with him until Elijah was taken up to heaven. When Elisha asked Elijah for a double portion of his spirit, he was expressing his desire to carry on Elijah's ministry.

LIVE IT OUT:
Show your loyalty to God through your actions every day.

Elisha Heals Naaman's Leprosy

2 Kings 5:1–10, 14

MEMORY VERSE:
But let him ask in faith, with no doubting, for he who doubts is like a wave of the sea driven and tossed by the wind.

—James 1:6

5 Now Naaman, commander of the army of the king of Syria, was a great and honorable man in the eyes of his master, because by him the Lord had given victory to Syria. He was also a mighty man of valor, but a leper. ²And the Syrians had gone out on raids, and had brought back captive a young girl from the land of Israel. She waited on Naaman's wife. ³Then she said to her mistress, "If only my master were with the prophet who is in Samaria! For he would heal him of his leprosy." ⁴And Naaman went in and told his master, saying, "Thus and thus said the girl who is from the land of Israel."

⁵Then the king of Syria said, "Go now, and I will send a letter to the king of Israel."

So he departed and took with him ten talents of silver, six thousand shekels of gold, and ten changes of clothing. ⁶Then he brought the letter to the king of Israel, which said,

"Now be advised, when this letter comes to you, that I have sent Naaman my servant to you, that you may heal him of his leprosy."

⁷And it happened, when the king of Israel read the letter, that he tore his clothes and said, "Am I God, to kill and make alive, that this man sends a man to me to heal him of his leprosy? Therefore please consider, and see how he seeks a quarrel with me."

⁸So it was, when Elisha the man of God heard that the king of Israel had torn his clothes, that he sent to the king, saying, "Why have you torn your clothes? Please let him come to me, and he shall know that there is a prophet in Israel."

⁹Then Naaman went with his horses and chariot, and he stood at the door of Elisha's house. ¹⁰And Elisha sent a messenger to him, saying, "Go and wash in the Jordan seven times, and your flesh shall be restored to you, and you shall be clean." . . .

This made Naaman very mad, because he thought Elisha should come out and heal him, so he left. But his servants convinced him to follow Elisha's message.

14So he went down and dipped seven times in the Jordan, according to the saying of the man of God; and his flesh was restored like the flesh of a little child, and he was clean. . . .

And then Naaman realized that there is no other God on earth except the God Elisha served.

DISCOVER:
Naaman was a mighty man who commanded a large army.
What was wrong with him?

UNDERSTAND:
The king of Israel complained when the king of Syria asked
him to help Naaman. Elisha was a man of God, and he
welcomed Naaman and treated him.

LIVE IT OUT:
Do you sometimes doubt your parents or teachers when they
want you to do things a certain way, and you think that your
way is better? Never doubt that God's way is the best way,
and pray for Him to lead you to make the right choices.

An Angel Army Fights for Elisha

2 Kings 6:8–12, 15–18, 21–22

MEMORY VERSE:
Though an army may encamp against me, my heart shall not fear; though war may rise against me, in this I will be confident.

—Psalm 27:3

6...⁸Now the king of Syria was making war against Israel; and he consulted with his servants, saying, "My camp will be in such and such a place." ⁹And the man of God sent to the king of Israel, saying, "Beware that you do not pass this place, for the Syrians are coming down there." ¹⁰Then the king of Israel sent someone to the place of which the man of God had told him. Thus he warned him, and he was watchful there, not just once or twice.

¹¹Therefore the heart of the king of Syria was greatly troubled by this thing; and he called his servants and said to them, "Will you not show me which of us is for the king of Israel?"

¹²And one of his servants said, "None, my lord, O king; but Elisha, the prophet who is in Israel, tells the king of Israel the words that you speak in your bedroom."...

So the king sent for Elisha.

131

¹⁵And when the servant of the man of God arose early and went out, there was an army, surrounding the city with horses and chariots. And his servant said to him, "Alas, my master! What shall we do?"

¹⁶So he answered, "Do not fear, for those who are with us are more than those who are with them." ¹⁷And Elisha prayed, and said, "LORD, I pray, open his eyes that he may see." Then the LORD opened the eyes of the young man, and he saw. And behold, the mountain was full of horses and chariots of fire all around Elisha. ¹⁸So when the Syrians came down to him, Elisha prayed to the LORD, and said, "Strike this people, I pray, with blindness." And He struck them with blindness according to the word of Elisha. . . .

Elisha then told them they were in the wrong city and led them to Samaria, where he prayed to the Lord to open their eyes.

²¹Now when the king of Israel saw them, he said to Elisha, "My father, shall I kill them? Shall I kill them?"

²²But he answered, "You shall not kill them. Would you kill those whom you have taken captive with your sword and your bow? Set food and water before them, that they may eat and drink and go to their master."

DISCOVER:

Why was Elisha not afraid when he awoke and the city was surrounded?

UNDERSTAND:

When the city was surrounded, Elisha's servants were afraid. Elisha was not afraid because he was working with God. He knew that God was all the help he needed.

LIVE IT OUT:

When we walk hand in hand with God, fear has no place in our lives.

An Eight-Year-Old King

2 Chronicles 34:1–2

MEMORY VERSE:
Do not turn to the right or the left; remove your foot from evil.

—Proverbs 4:27

34 Josiah was eight years old when he became king, and he reigned thirty-one years in Jerusalem. ²And he did what was right in the sight of the LORD, and walked in the ways of his father David; he did not turn aside to the right hand or to the left.

DISCOVER:
How old was Josiah when he became king? How long was he king?

UNDERSTAND:
Josiah lived by the Lord's Word and always did what was right.

LIVE IT OUT:
Every day we should walk in the ways of the Lord and do only good things.

BEAUTIFUL QUEEN ESTHER

Esther 2:7–12, 15–18

MEMORY VERSE:
...And Esther obtained favor in the sight of all who saw her.

—*Esther 12:15b*

2 ...⁷And Mordecai had brought up Hadassah, that is, Esther, his uncle's daughter, for she had neither father nor mother. The young woman was lovely and beautiful. When her father and mother died, Mordecai took her as his own daughter.

⁸So it was, when the king's command and decree were heard, and when many young women were gathered at Shushan the citadel, under the custody of Hegai, that Esther also was taken to the king's palace, into the care of Hegai the custodian of the women. ⁹Now the young woman pleased him, and she obtained his favor; so he readily gave beauty preparations to her, besides her allowance. Then seven choice maidservants were provided for her from the king's palace, and he moved her and her maidservants to the best place in the house of the women.

¹⁰Esther had not revealed her people or family, for Mordecai had charged her not to reveal it. ¹¹And every day Mordecai paced in front of the court of the women's quarters, to learn of Esther's welfare and what was happening to her.

^{12}Each young woman's turn came to go in to King Ahasuerus after she had completed twelve months' preparation, according to the regulations for the women, for thus were the days of their preparation apportioned: six months with oil of myrrh, and six months with perfumes and preparations for beautifying women. . . .

^{15}Now when the turn came for Esther the daughter of Abihail the uncle of Mordecai, who had taken her as his daughter, to go in to the king, she requested nothing but what Hegai the king's eunuch, the custodian of the women, advised. And Esther obtained favor in the sight of all who saw her. ^{16}So Esther was taken to King Ahasuerus, into his royal palace, in the tenth month, which is the

month of Tebeth, in the seventh year of his reign. [17]The king loved Esther more than all the other women, and she obtained grace and favor in his sight more than all the virgins; so he set the royal crown upon her head and made her queen instead of Vashti. [18]Then the king made a great feast, the Feast of Esther, for all his officials and servants; and he proclaimed a holiday in the provinces and gave gifts according to the generosity of a king.

DISCOVER:
How long did it take for Esther to get ready to meet the king?

UNDERSTAND:
Esther followed Hegai's advice when she was presented to King Ahasuerus, and he chose her to be queen.

LIVE IT OUT:
When we listen to and follow God's instructions, He will guide us to the right choice.

SATAN TESTS JOB

Job 1:1–3; 2:1–10

MEMORY VERSE:
But He knows the way that I take; when He has tested me,
I shall come forth as gold. My foot has held fast to His
steps; I have kept His way and not turned aside.

—Job 23:10–11

1There was a man in the land of Uz, whose name was Job; and that man was blameless and upright, and one who feared God and shunned evil. 2And seven sons and three daughters were born to him. 3Also, his possessions were seven thousand sheep, three thousand camels, five hundred yoke of oxen, five hundred female donkeys, and a very large household, so that this man was the greatest of all the people of the East....

2Again there was a day when the sons of God came to present themselves before the Lord, and Satan came also among them to present himself before the Lord. 2And the Lord said to Satan, "From where do you come?"

Satan answered the Lord and said, "From going to and fro on the earth, and from walking back and forth on it."

³Then the LORD said to Satan, "Have you considered My servant Job, that there is none like him on the earth, a blameless and upright man, one who fears God and shuns evil? And still he holds fast to his integrity, although you incited Me against him, to destroy him without cause."

⁴So Satan answered the LORD and said, "Skin for skin! Yes, all that a man has he will give for his life. ⁵But stretch out Your hand now, and touch his bone and his flesh, and he will surely curse You to Your face!"

⁶And the LORD said to Satan, "Behold, he is in your hand, but spare his life."

⁷So Satan went out from the presence of the LORD, and struck Job with painful boils from the sole of his foot to the crown of his head. ⁸And he took for himself a potsherd with which to scrape himself while he sat in the midst of the ashes.

⁹Then his wife said to him, "Do you still hold fast to your integrity? Curse God and die!"

¹⁰But he said to her, "You speak as one of the foolish women speaks. Shall we indeed accept good from God, and shall we not accept adversity?" In all this Job did not sin with his lips.

DISCOVER:

Who put sores on Job's body? When the sons of God went to see the Lord, who came with them?

UNDERSTAND:

Job was very sick, but he did not blame God. All of his life, Job loved God and never turned away from Him.

LIVE IT OUT:

We should live our lives so that our friends know we are God's children.

THE BLAZING FURNACE

Daniel 3:13–25

MEMORY VERSE:
I will call upon the LORD, who is worthy to be praised; so
shall I be saved from my enemies.

—Psalm 18:3

3... ¹³Then Nebuchadnezzar, in rage and fury, gave the command to bring Shadrach, Meshach, and Abed-Nego. So they brought these men before the king. ¹⁴Nebuchadnezzar spoke, saying to them, "Is it true, Shadrach, Meshach, and Abed-Nego, that you do not serve my gods or worship the gold image which I have set up? ¹⁵Now if you are ready at the time you hear the sound of the horn, flute, harp, lyre, and psaltery, in symphony with all kinds of music, and you fall down and worship the image which I have made, good! But if you do not worship, you shall be cast immediately into the midst of a burning fiery furnace. And who is the god who will deliver you from my hands?"

¹⁶Shadrach, Meshach, and Abed-Nego answered and said to the king, "O Nebuchadnezzar, we have no need to answer you in this matter. ¹⁷If that is the case, our God whom we serve is able to deliver us from the burning fiery furnace, and He will deliver us from your hand, O king. ¹⁸But if not, let it be known to you, O king, that we do not serve your gods, nor will we worship the gold image which you have set up."

¹⁹Then Nebuchadnezzar was full of fury, and the expression on his face changed toward Shadrach, Meshach, and Abed-Nego. He spoke and commanded that they heat the furnace seven times more than it was usually heated. ²⁰And he commanded certain mighty men of valor who were in his army to bind Shadrach, Meshach, and Abed-Nego, and cast them into the burning fiery furnace. ²¹Then these men were bound in their coats, their trousers, their turbans, and their other garments, and were cast into the midst of the burning fiery furnace. ²²Therefore, because the king's command was urgent, and the furnace exceedingly hot, the flame of the fire killed those men who took up Shadrach, Meshach, and Abed-Nego.

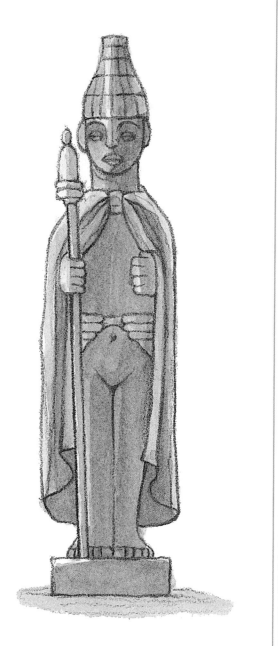

²³And these three men, Shadrach, Meshach, and Abed-Nego, fell down bound into the midst of the burning fiery furnace.

²⁴Then King Nebuchadnezzar was astonished; and he rose in haste and spoke, saying to his counselors, "Did we not cast three men bound into the midst of the fire?"

They answered and said to the king, "True, O king."

²⁵"Look!" he answered, "I see four men loose, walking in the midst of the fire; and they are not hurt, and the form of the fourth is like the Son of God."

DISCOVER:
Why did King Nebuchadnezzar send the three men into the furnace? Who was the fourth man King Nebuchadnezzar saw walking around in the blazing furnace?

UNDERSTAND:
Shadrach, Meshach, and Abed-Nego showed their faith in God when they told King Nebuchadnezzar that he could throw them into the blazing furnace.

LIVE IT OUT:
Every day our faith in God is tested. We must hold fast and know that our faith will be rewarded.

KING NEBUCHADNEZZAR EATS GRASS

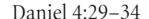

Daniel 4:29–34

MEMORY VERSE:
"And whoever exalts himself will be humbled, and he who humbles himself will be exalted."
—*Matthew 23:12*

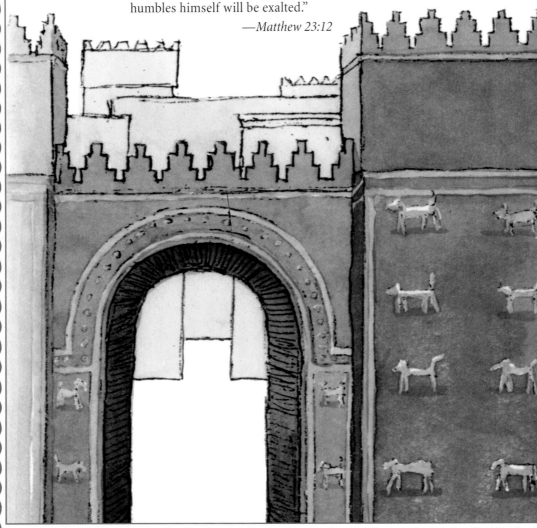

4 …²⁹At the end of the twelve months he was walking about the royal palace of Babylon. ³⁰The king spoke, saying, "Is not this great Babylon, that I have built for a royal dwelling by my mighty power and for the honor of my majesty?"

³¹While the word was still in the king's mouth, a voice fell from heaven: "King Nebuchadnezzar, to you it is spoken: the kingdom has departed from you! ³²And they shall drive you from men, and your

dwelling shall be with the beasts of the field. They shall make you eat grass like oxen; and seven times shall pass over you, until you know that the Most High rules in the kingdom of men, and gives it to whomever He chooses."

³³That very hour the word was fulfilled concerning Nebuchadnezzar; he was driven from men and ate grass like oxen; his body was wet with the dew of heaven till his hair had grown like eagles' feathers and his nails like birds' claws.

³⁴"And at the end of the time I, Nebuchadnezzar, lifted my eyes to heaven, and my understanding returned to me; and I blessed the Most High and praised and honored Him who lives forever:

"For His dominion is an everlasting dominion, and His kingdom is from generation to generation."

DISCOVER:
When King Nebuchadnezzar boasted about his greatness, what did the Lord do to show King Nebuchadnezzar how to be humble?

UNDERSTAND:
God knew that King Nebuchadnezzar was feeling too self-important. For seven years, God made the king live out in the fields and eat grass like an animal. When King Nebuchadnezzar understood he should be humble and that no man is greater than God, King Nebuchadnezzar praised God.

LIVE IT OUT:
We praise God and honor Him by the things we say and do.

Daniel in the Lions' Den

Daniel 6:1–3, 5, 10, 18–22

MEMORY VERSE:

But You, O LORD, are a shield for me, my glory and the One who lifts up my head.

—Psalm 3:3

6 It pleased Darius to set over the kingdom one hundred and twenty satraps, to be over the whole kingdom; ²and over these, three governors, of whom Daniel was one, that the satraps might give account to them, so that the king would suffer no loss. ³Then this Daniel distinguished himself above the governors and satraps, because an excellent spirit was in him; and the king gave thought to setting him over the whole realm.

The governors and satraps were jealous of Daniel, but they could not find any charge to bring against him.

⁵Then these men said, "We shall not find any charge against this Daniel unless we find it against him concerning the law of his God." . . .

So these men convinced the king to establish a law that every man who prayed to a god or a man other than the king would be cast into the lions' den. And the king signed the law, not realizing that he had been tricked.

10Now when Daniel knew that the writing was signed, he went home. And in his upper room, with his windows open toward Jerusalem, he knelt down on his knees three times that day, and prayed and gave thanks before his God, as was his custom since early days. . . .

When these men found Daniel praying they went before the king and reminded him of the decree he had signed. The king was displeased with himself, but he could think of no way to save Daniel. And when the men returned, the king gave the order and they brought Daniel and cast him into the den of lions.

¹⁸Now the king went to his palace and spent the night fasting; and no musicians were brought before him. Also his sleep went from him. ¹⁹Then the king arose very early in the morning and went in haste to the den of lions. ²⁰And when he came to the den, he cried out with a lamenting voice to Daniel. The king spoke, saying to Daniel, "Daniel, servant of the living God, has your God, whom you serve continually, been able to deliver you from the lions?"

²¹Then Daniel said to the king, "O king, live forever! ²²My God sent His angel and shut the lions' mouths, so that they have not hurt me, because I was found innocent before Him; and also, O king, I have done no wrong before you." . . .

The king was very glad that Daniel was safe, and he ordered that Daniel be removed from the lions' den. When Daniel was brought out, they saw that because of his belief in God, he had not been harmed.

DISCOVER:
How did God keep the lions from harming Daniel?

UNDERSTAND:
Daniel prayed to God three times a day. Daniel was saved from the lions because he trusted in God.

LIVE IT OUT:
Serve God faithfully, as Daniel did, and He will protect you.

WHY THE FISH SWALLOWED JONAH

Jonah 1:1–5, 7, 12, 15, 17; 2:1—3:3a

MEMORY VERSE:
"For there is nothing covered that will not be revealed, and hidden that will not be known."

—*Matthew 10:26b*

1Now the word of the LORD came to Jonah the son of Amittai, saying, 2"Arise, go to Nineveh, that great city, and cry out against it; for their wickedness has come up before Me."

3But Jonah arose to flee to Tarshish from the presence of the LORD. He went down to Joppa, and found a ship going to Tarshish; so he paid the fare, and went down into it, to go with them to Tarshish from the presence of the LORD.

4But the LORD sent out a great wind on the sea, and there was a mighty tempest on the sea, so that the ship was about to be broken up. 5Then the mariners were afraid. . . . 7And they said to one another, "Come, let us cast lots, that we may know for whose cause this trouble has come upon us." So they cast lots, and the lot fell on Jonah. . . .

12And he said to them, "Pick me up and throw me into the sea; then the sea will become calm for you. For I know that this great tempest is because of me." . . .

15So they picked up Jonah and threw him into the sea, and the sea ceased from its raging. . . .

¹⁷Now the Lᴏʀᴅ had prepared a great fish to swallow Jonah. And Jonah was in the belly of the fish three days and three nights.

2Then Jonah prayed to the Lᴏʀᴅ his God from the fish's belly. ²And he said:

"I cried out to the Lᴏʀᴅ because of my affliction, and He answered me.

"Out of the belly of Sheol I cried, and You heard my voice. ³For You cast me into the deep, into the heart of the seas, and the floods surrounded me; all Your billows and Your waves passed over me.

⁴Then I said, 'I have been cast out of Your sight; yet I will look again toward Your holy temple.' ⁵The waters surrounded me, even to my soul; the deep closed around me; weeds were wrapped around my head. ⁶I went down to the moorings of the mountains; the earth with its bars closed behind me forever; yet You have brought up my life from the pit, O LORD, my God.

⁷"When my soul fainted within me, I remembered the LORD; and my prayer went up to You, into Your holy temple.

⁸"Those who regard worthless idols forsake their own Mercy. ⁹But I will sacrifice to You with the voice of thanksgiving; I will pay what I have vowed. Salvation is of the LORD."

¹⁰So the LORD spoke to the fish, and it vomited Jonah onto dry land.

3 Now the word of the LORD came to Jonah the second time, saying, ²"Arise, go to Nineveh, that great city, and preach to it the message that I tell you." ³So Jonah arose and went to Nineveh, according to the word of the LORD.

DISCOVER:
Where did Jonah try to hide from the Lord? What happened when the men threw Jonah into the sea? How long was Jonah in the belly of the fish?

UNDERSTAND:
Jonah tried to hide from the Lord, but the Lord knew where Jonah was all the time. The Lord had the fish swallow Jonah so Jonah would know God was in control and that he could not hide from the Lord. No one can hide from the Lord.

LIVE IT OUT:
Since the Lord is always with us, He sees everything we do—good or bad.

WISE MEN FOLLOW A STAR

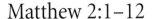

Matthew 2:1–12

MEMORY VERSE:
For unto us a Child is born, unto us a Son is given; and the government will be upon His shoulder. And His name will be called Wonderful, Counselor, Mighty God, Everlasting Father, Prince of Peace.

—Isaiah 9:6

2 Now after Jesus was born in Bethlehem of Judea in the days of Herod the king, wise men from the East came to Jerusalem, ²saying, "Where is He who has been born King of the Jews? For we have seen His star in the East and have come to worship Him."

³When Herod the king heard this, he was troubled, and all Jerusalem with him. ⁴And when he had gathered all the chief priests and scribes of the people together, he inquired of them where the Christ was to be born.

⁵So they said to him, "In Bethlehem of Judea, for thus it is written by the prophet:

⁶"But you, Bethlehem, in the land of Judah, are not the least among the rulers of Judah; for out of you shall come a Ruler who will shepherd My people Israel.'"

⁷Then Herod, when he had secretly called the wise men, determined from them what time the star appeared. ⁸And he sent them to Bethlehem and said, "Go and search carefully for the young Child, and when you have found Him, bring back word to me, that I may come and worship Him also."

⁹When they heard the king, they departed; and behold, the star which they had seen in the East went before them, till it came and stood over where the young Child was. ¹⁰When they saw the star, they rejoiced with exceedingly great joy. ¹¹And when they had come into the house, they saw the young Child with Mary His mother, and fell down and worshiped Him. And when they had opened their treasures, they presented gifts to Him: gold, frankincense, and myrrh.

¹²Then, being divinely warned in a dream that they should not return to Herod, they departed for their own country another way.

DISCOVER:
How were the wise men guided to the baby Jesus?

UNDERSTAND:
When the wise men saw the Child they gave Him gifts and worshiped Him. God warned the wise men not to go back to King Herod. They took his warning seriously and returned home another way.

LIVE IT OUT:
Spend time every day in prayer, praising God for His wonderful Son, our Savior.

An Angel Warns Joseph

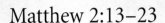

Matthew 2:13–23

MEMORY VERSE:
For this is God, our God forever and ever; He will be our
guide even to death.

—*Psalm 48:14*

2... ¹³Now when they had departed, behold, an angel of the Lord
appeared to Joseph in a dream, saying, "Arise, take the young Child
and His mother, flee to Egypt, and stay there until I bring you word; for
Herod will seek the young Child to destroy Him."

¹⁴When he arose, he took the young Child and His
mother by night and departed for Egypt, ¹⁵and
was there until the death of Herod, that it

might be fulfilled which was spoken by the Lord through the prophet, saying, "Out of Egypt I called My Son."

16Then Herod, when he saw that he was deceived by the wise men, was exceedingly angry; and he sent forth and put to death all the male children who were in Bethlehem and in all its districts, from two years old and under, according to the time which he had determined from the wise men. 17Then was fulfilled what was spoken by Jeremiah the prophet, saying:

18"A voice was heard in Ramah, lamentation, weeping, and great mourning, Rachel weeping for her children, refusing to be comforted, because they are no more."

19Now when Herod was dead, behold, an angel of the Lord appeared in a dream to Joseph in Egypt, 20saying, "Arise, take the young Child and His mother, and go to the land of Israel, for those who sought the young Child's life are dead." 21Then he arose, took the young Child and His mother, and came into the land of Israel.

22But when he heard that Archelaus was reigning over Judea instead of his father Herod, he was afraid to go there. And being warned by God in a dream, he turned aside into the region of Galilee. 23And he came and dwelt in a city called Nazareth, that it might be fulfilled which was spoken by the prophets, "He shall be called a Nazarene."

DISCOVER:
What did the angel of the Lord tell Joseph to do?

UNDERSTAND:
King Herod gave an order to kill all the baby boys in Bethlehem two years old and younger. He did this because he was afraid Jesus would replace him as king. Because Mary, Joseph, and Jesus fled to Egypt, Jesus lived.

LIVE IT OUT:
Joseph trusted the angel of the Lord and did what he was told. Listen carefully to the commands God has given us and do your best to follow those commands every day.

The Good Seed

Matthew 13:1–9, 18–23

MEMORY VERSE:
"I am the vine, you are the branches. He who abides in Me, and I in him, bears much fruit; for without Me you can do nothing."

—John 15:5

13 ①n the same day Jesus went out of the house and sat by the sea. ²And great multitudes were gathered together to Him, so that He got into a boat and sat; and the whole multitude stood on the shore.

³Then He spoke many things to them in parables, saying: "Behold, a sower went out to sow. ⁴And as he sowed, some seed fell by the wayside; and the birds came and devoured them. ⁵Some fell on stony places, where they did not have much earth; and they immediately sprang up because they had no depth of earth.⁶But when the sun was up they were scorched, and because they had no root they withered away. ⁷And some fell among thorns, and the thorns sprang up and choked them. ⁸But others fell on good ground and yielded a crop: some a hundredfold, some sixty, some thirty. ⁹He who has ears to hear, let him hear!"…

¹⁸"Therefore hear the parable of the sower: ¹⁹When anyone hears the word of the kingdom, and does not understand it, then the wicked one comes and snatches away what was sown in his heart. This is he who received seed by the wayside. ²⁰But he who received the seed on stony places, this is he who hears the word and immediately receives it with joy; ²¹yet he has no root in himself, but endures only for a while. For when tribulation or persecution arises because of the word, immediately he stumbles. ²²Now he who received seed among the thorns is

he who hears the word, and the cares of this world and the deceitfulness of riches choke the word, and he becomes unfruitful. [23]But he who received seed on the good ground is he who hears the word and understands it, who indeed bears fruit and produces: some a hundredfold, some sixty, some thirty."

DISCOVER:

Why did Jesus speak in parables?

UNDERSTAND:

Parables are stories that teach a religious principle or a moral lesson. Jesus sometimes used parables in his teachings so His followers could better understand how to live as God desires.

LIVE IT OUT:

God wants us all to be like the seed planted on good ground so that we will hear and understand His Word. To do this, we must study the Bible.

JESUS WALKS ON WATER

Matthew 14:22–33

MEMORY VERSE:

Behold, God is my salvation, I will trust and not be afraid . . .

—Isaiah 12:2

14. . . ²²Immediately Jesus made His disciples get into the boat and go before Him to the other side, while He sent the multitudes away. ²³And when He had sent the multitudes away, He went up on the mountain by Himself to pray. Now when evening came, He was alone there. ²⁴But the boat was now in the middle of the sea, tossed by the waves, for the wind was contrary.

²⁵Now in the fourth watch of the night Jesus went to them, walking on the sea. ²⁶And when the disciples saw Him walking on the sea, they were troubled, saying, "It is a ghost!" And they cried out for fear.

²⁷But immediately Jesus spoke to them, saying, "Be of good cheer! It is I; do not be afraid."

²⁸And Peter answered Him and said, "Lord, if it is You, command me to come to You on the water."

²⁹So He said, "Come." And when Peter had come down out of the boat, he walked on the water to go to Jesus. ³⁰But when he saw that the wind was boisterous, he was afraid; and beginning to sink he cried out, saying, "Lord, save me!"

³¹And immediately Jesus stretched out His hand and caught him, and said to him, "O you of little faith, why did you doubt?" ³²And when they got into the boat, the wind ceased.

³³Then those who were in the boat came and worshiped Him, saying, "Truly You are the Son of God."

DISCOVER:

What did the disciples who were in the boat say to Jesus after he calmed the storm?

UNDERSTAND:

Jesus was alone on the mountain, but the boat was in the middle of the sea. When the disciples saw him walking on the water, they thought he was a ghost! But Jesus spoke to them and said, "Be of good cheer! It is I; do not be afraid."

LIVE IT OUT:

Jesus stretches out His hand to us. He is our salvation. Never doubt Him.

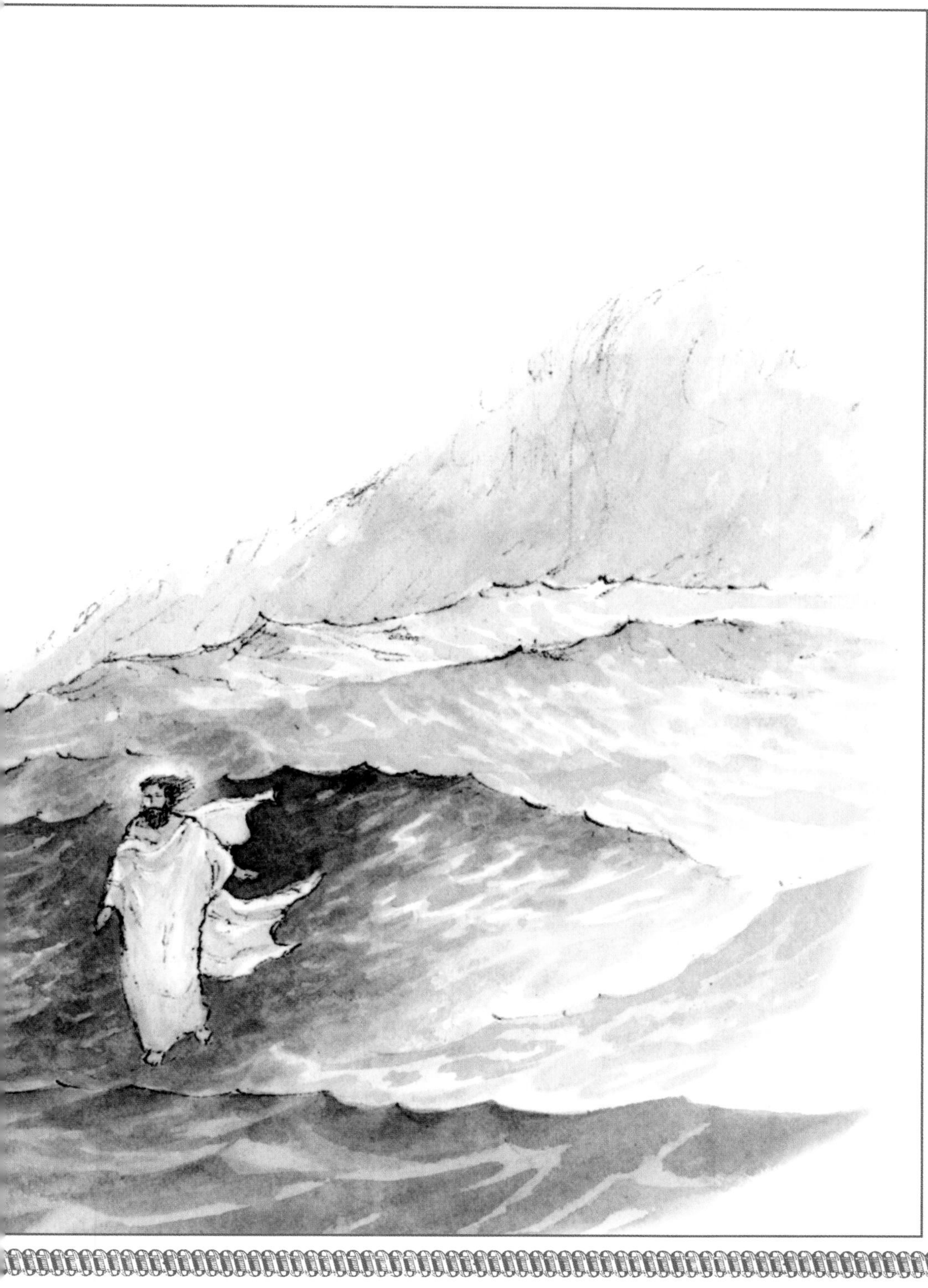

A House of Prayer

Matthew 21:1–17

MEMORY VERSE:
"Fear not, daughter of Zion; behold, your King is coming, sitting on a donkey's colt."

—*John 12:15*

1Now when they drew near Jerusalem, and came to Bethphage, at the Mount of Olives, then Jesus sent two disciples, 2saying to them, "Go into the village opposite you, and immediately you will find a donkey tied, and a colt with her. Loose them and bring them to Me. 3And if anyone says anything to you, you shall say, 'The Lord has need of them,' and immediately he will send them."

4All this was done that it might be fulfilled which was spoken by the prophet, saying:

5"Tell the daughter of Zion, 'Behold, your King is coming to you, lowly, and sitting on a donkey, a colt, the foal of a donkey.'"

6So the disciples went and did as Jesus commanded them. 7They brought the donkey

and the colt, laid their clothes on them, and set Him on them. ⁸And a very great multitude spread their clothes on the road; others cut down branches from the trees and spread them on the road. ⁹Then the multitudes who went before and those who followed cried out, saying:

"Hosanna to the Son of David!

'Blessed is He who comes in the name of the Lᴏʀᴅ!'
Hosanna in the highest!"

¹⁰And when He had come into Jerusalem, all the city was moved, saying, "Who is this?"

¹¹So the multitudes said, "This is Jesus, the prophet from Nazareth of Galilee."

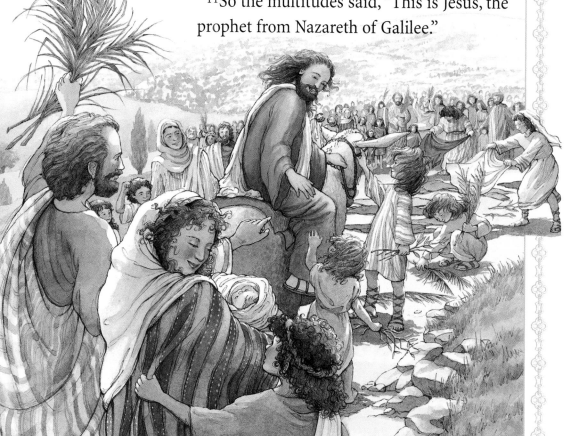

¹²Then Jesus went into the temple of God and drove out all those who bought and sold in the temple, and overturned the tables of the money changers and the seats of those who sold doves. ¹³And He said to them, "It is written, 'My house shall be called a house of prayer,' but you have made it a 'den of thieves.'"

¹⁴Then the blind and the lame came to Him in the temple, and He healed them. ¹⁵But when the chief priests and scribes saw the wonderful things that He did, and the children crying out in the temple and saying, "Hosanna to the Son of David!" they were indignant ¹⁶and said to Him, "Do You hear what these are saying?"

And Jesus said to them, "Yes. Have you never read,

'Out of the mouth of babes and nursing infants you have perfected praise'?"

¹⁷Then He left them and went out of the city to Bethany, and He lodged there.

DISCOVER:
What did Jesus command his disciples to do? Why?

UNDERSTAND:
When Jesus went into the temple of God, he saw a lot of sinful things happening. This made Him very unhappy, and He sent out the people who were dishonoring His house of prayer. Then He healed the blind and the lame.

LIVE IT OUT:
We should always be mindful of God's presence in our lives, whether in our places of worship or in our own backyard.

A Disciple Denies Jesus

Matthew 26:57–60, 69–75

MEMORY VERSE:
"But whoever denies Me before men, him I will also deny before My Father who is in heaven."

—*Matthew 10:33*

26 ...⁵⁷And those who had laid hold of Jesus led Him away to Caiaphas the high priest, where the scribes and the elders were assembled. ⁵⁸But Peter followed Him at a distance to the high priest's courtyard. And he went in and sat with the servants to see the end.

⁵⁹Now the chief priests, the elders, and all the council sought false testimony against Jesus to put Him to death, ⁶⁰but found none....

⁶⁹Now Peter sat outside in the courtyard. And a servant girl came to him, saying, "You also were with Jesus of Galilee."

⁷⁰But he denied it before them all, saying, "I do not know what you are saying."

⁷¹And when he had gone out to the gateway, another girl saw him and said to those who were there, "This fellow also was with Jesus of Nazareth."

⁷²But again he denied with an oath, "I do not know the Man!"

⁷³And a little later those who stood by came up and said to Peter, "Surely you also are one of them, for your speech betrays you."

⁷⁴Then he began to curse and swear, saying, "I do not know the Man!"

Immediately a rooster crowed. ⁷⁵And Peter remembered the word of Jesus who had said to him, "Before the rooster crows, you will deny Me three times." So he went out and wept bitterly.

DISCOVER:
What did Peter say when asked if he was with Jesus?

UNDERSTAND:
Peter wept bitterly when he heard the rooster crow and remembered the word of Jesus: "Before the rooster crows, you will deny Me three times."

LIVE IT OUT:
We can be a true witness for the Lord in all we do. We should always be ready to say we are followers of Jesus.

JESUS CALMS THE STORM

Mark 4:35–41

MEMORY VERSE:
The fear of man brings a snare, but whoever trusts in the
LORD shall be safe.

—*Proverbs 29:25*

4... ³⁵On the same day, when evening had come, He said to them,
"Let us cross over to the other side." ³⁶Now when they had left the
multitude, they took Him along in the boat as He was. And other little
boats were also with Him. ³⁷And a great windstorm arose, and the

waves beat into the boat, so that it was already filling. [38]But He was in the stern, asleep on a pillow. And they awoke Him and said to Him, "Teacher, do You not care that we are perishing?"

[39]Then He arose and rebuked the wind, and said to the sea, "Peace, be still!" And the wind ceased and there was a great calm. [40]But He said to them, "Why are you so fearful? How is it that you have no faith?" [41]And they feared exceedingly, and said to one another, "Who can this be, that even the wind and the sea obey Him!"

DISCOVER:

Where was Jesus when the great windstorm struck? What was He doing?

UNDERSTAND:

After Jesus calmed the sea, He asked, "Why are you so fearful?" But the people feared even more and wondered what type of person could make the wind and sea obey Him.

LIVE IT OUT:

When we trust in the Lord, He will keep us safe.

JESUS FEEDS THE MULTITUDES

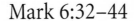

Mark 6:32–44

MEMORY VERSE:
Through the LORD's mercies we are not consumed,
because His compassions fail not.

—*Lamentations 3:22*

6 ... ³²So they departed to a deserted place in the boat by themselves.

³³But the multitudes saw them departing, and many knew Him and ran there on foot from all the cities. They arrived before them and came together to Him.

³⁴And Jesus, when He came out, saw a great multitude and was moved with compassion for them, because they were like sheep not having a shepherd. So He began to teach them many things. ³⁵When the day was now far spent, His disciples came to Him and said, "This is a deserted place, and already the hour is late. ³⁶Send them away, that they may go into the surrounding country and villages and buy themselves bread; for they have nothing to eat."

³⁷But He answered and said to them, "You give them something to eat."

And they said to Him, "Shall we go and buy two hundred denarii worth of bread and give them something to eat?"

³⁸But He said to them, "How many loaves do you have? Go and see."

And when they found out they said, "Five, and two fish."

³⁹Then He commanded them to make them all sit down in groups on the green grass. ⁴⁰So they sat down in ranks, in hundreds and in fifties. ⁴¹And when He had taken the five loaves and the two fish, He looked up to heaven, blessed and broke the loaves, and gave them to His disciples to set before them; and the two fish He divided among them all. ⁴²So they all ate and were filled. ⁴³And they took up twelve baskets full of fragments and of the fish. ⁴⁴Now those who had eaten the loaves were about five thousand men.

DISCOVER:
How many loaves of bread and how many fish did Jesus' disciples have with them? How many people did Jesus feed?

UNDERSTAND:
Jesus looked up to heaven, blessed and broke the bread and fish, and divided it among all the people. Even after feeding five thousand people, there were twelve baskets of food left over!

LIVE IT OUT:
God always provides for our needs. Remember to thank God for everything He gives us.

LET THE CHILDREN COME

Mark 10:13–16

MEMORY VERSE:
But as many as received Him, to them He gave the right to
become children of God, to those who believe in His
name.

—John 1:12

10... ¹³Then they brought little children to Him, that He might
touch them; but the disciples rebuked those who brought them. ¹⁴But
when Jesus saw it, He was greatly displeased and said to them, "Let the
little children come to Me, and do not forbid them; for of such is the
kingdom of God. ¹⁵Assuredly, I say to you, whoever does not receive
the kingdom of God as a little child will by no means enter it."
¹⁶And He took them up in His arms, laid His hands on them, and
blessed them.

DISCOVER:

Why did people bring their children to Jesus?

UNDERSTAND:

Jesus said the kingdom of God belongs to those who receive it like little children. This means we must accept the kingdom of God wholeheartedly, cheerfully, and totally.

LIVE IT OUT:

No matter what age we are, we can come to Jesus like little children do—with open hearts and minds—to receive His blessings.

THE LORD'S SUPPER

Mark 14:12-26

MEMORY VERSE:

Then He said to them, "With fervent desire I have desired to eat this Passover with you before I suffer; for I say to you, I will no longer eat of it until it is fulfilled in the kingdom of God."

—*Luke 22:15-16*

14...¹²Now on the first day of Unleavened Bread, when they killed the Passover lamb, His disciples said to Him, "Where do You want us to go and prepare, that You may eat the Passover?"

¹³And He sent out two of His disciples and said to them, "Go into the city, and a man will meet you carrying a pitcher of water; follow him. ¹⁴Wherever he goes in, say to the master of the house, 'The Teacher says, "Where is the guest room in which I may eat the Passover with My disciples?" ' ¹⁵Then he will show you a large upper room, furnished and prepared; there make ready for us."

¹⁶So His disciples went out, and came into the city, and found it just as He had said to them; and they prepared the Passover.

¹⁷In the evening He came with the twelve. ¹⁸Now as they sat and ate, Jesus said, "Assuredly, I say to you, one of you who eats with Me will betray Me."

¹⁹And they began to be sorrowful, and to say to Him one by one, "Is it I?" And another said, "Is it I?"

²⁰He answered and said to them, "It is one of the twelve, who dips with Me in the dish. ²¹The Son of Man indeed goes just as it is written of Him, but woe to that man by whom the Son of Man is betrayed! It would have been good for that man if he had never been born."

²²And as they were eating, Jesus took bread, blessed and broke it, and gave it to them and said, "Take, eat; this is My body."

²³Then He took the cup, and when He had given thanks He gave it to them, and they all drank from it. ²⁴And He said to them, "This is My blood of the new covenant, which is shed for many. ²⁵Assuredly, I say to you, I will no longer drink of the fruit of the vine until that day when I drink it new in the kingdom of God."

²⁶And when they had sung a hymn, they went out to the Mount of Olives.

DISCOVER:

What did Jesus' followers say when Jesus told them that one of the twelve disciples would betray Him?

UNDERSTAND:

The bread was a symbol for Jesus' body, and the wine a symbol for His blood, which He would shed on the cross, a sacrifice that would save us.

LIVE IT OUT:

Jesus shed His blood for us so that we may have everlasting life. Always remember His sacrifice. He did it for you.

THE BOY JESUS LINGERS IN THE TEMPLE

Luke 2:39–52

MEMORY VERSE:
"But you, do not be called 'Rabbi'; for One is your Teacher,
the Christ, and you are all brethren."

—*Matthew 23:8*

2 ... ³⁹So when they had performed all things according to the law of the Lord, they returned to Galilee, to their own city, Nazareth. ⁴⁰And the Child grew and became strong in spirit, filled with wisdom; and the grace of God was upon Him.

⁴¹His parents went to Jerusalem every year at the Feast of the Passover. ⁴²And when He was twelve years old, they went up to Jerusalem according to the custom of the feast. ⁴³When they had finished the days, as they returned, the Boy Jesus lingered behind in Jerusalem. And Joseph and His mother did not know it; ⁴⁴but supposing Him to have been in the company, they went a day's journey, and sought Him among their relatives and acquaintances. ⁴⁵So when they did not find Him, they returned to Jerusalem, seeking Him.

⁴⁶Now so it was that after three days they found Him in the temple, sitting in the midst of the teachers, both listening to them and asking

them questions. ⁴⁷And all who heard Him were astonished at His understanding and answers. ⁴⁸So when they saw Him, they were amazed; and His mother said to Him, "Son, why have You done this to us? Look, Your father and I have sought You anxiously."

⁴⁹And He said to them, "Why did you seek Me? Did you not know that I must be about My Father's business?" ⁵⁰But they did not understand the statement which He spoke to them.

⁵¹Then He went down with them and came to Nazareth, and was subject to them, but His mother kept all these things in her heart. ⁵²And Jesus increased in wisdom and stature, and in favor with God and men.

DISCOVER:
Where did Mary and Joseph find Jesus? What was he doing?

UNDERSTAND:
Even though he was only twelve years old, Jesus was doing the work of His heavenly Father, listening to the teachers in the temple and asking questions.

LIVE IT OUT:
No matter how young or old we are, we are able to do the work of God.

John Baptizes Jesus

Luke 3:1–6, 15–18, 21–22

MEMORY VERSE:
And suddenly a voice came from heaven, saying, "This is
My beloved Son, in whom I am well pleased."

—*Matthew 3:17*

3 Now in the fifteenth year of the reign of Tiberius Caesar, Pontius Pilate being governor of Judea, Herod being tetrarch of Galilee, his brother Philip tetrarch of Iturea and the region of Trachonitis, and Lysanias tetrarch of Abilene, 2while Annas and Caiaphas were high priests, the word of God came to John the son of Zacharias in the

wilderness. ³And he went into all the region around the Jordan, preaching a baptism of repentance for the remission of sins, ⁴as it is written in the book of the words of Isaiah the prophet, saying:

"The voice of one crying in the wilderness: 'Prepare the way of the Lord; Make His paths straight. ⁵Every valley shall be filled and every mountain and hill brought low; the crooked places shall be made straight and the rough ways smooth; ⁶and all flesh shall see the salvation of God.' ". . .

¹⁵Now as the people were in expectation, and all reasoned in their hearts about John, whether he was the Christ or not, ¹⁶John answered, saying to all, "I indeed baptize you with water; but One mightier than I is coming, whose sandal strap I am not worthy to loose. He will baptize you with the Holy Spirit and fire. ¹⁷His winnowing fan is in His hand, and He will thoroughly clean out His threshing floor, and gather the wheat into His barn; but the chaff He will burn with unquenchable fire."

¹⁸And with many other exhortations he preached to the people. . . .

²¹When all the people were baptized, it came to pass that Jesus also was baptized; and while He prayed, the heaven was opened. ²²And the Holy Spirit descended in bodily form like a dove upon Him, and a voice came from heaven which said, "You are My beloved Son; in You I am well pleased."

DISCOVER:

What message did John the Baptist preach to the people?
Why is he called John the Baptist?

UNDERSTAND:

John baptized many people, and then he baptized Jesus.
After he was baptized, Jesus prayed. The heavens opened and
the Holy Spirit came down upon him in the form of a dove.
Then God's voice came from heaven, saying, "You are My
Beloved Son; in you I am well pleased.

LIVE IT OUT:

Follow God's instructions for living a Christian life, and He
will be pleased.

The Great Catch

Luke 5:1–11

MEMORY VERSE:
Then He said to them, "Follow Me, and I will make you fishers of men."

—*Matthew 4:19*

5 So it was, as the multitude pressed about Him to hear the word of God, that He stood by the Lake of Gennesaret,

²and saw two boats standing by the lake; but the fishermen had gone from them and were washing their nets. ³Then He got into one of the boats, which was Simon's, and asked him to put out a little from the land. And He sat down and taught the multitudes from the boat.

⁴When He had stopped speaking, He said to Simon, "Launch out into the deep and let down your nets for a catch."

⁵But Simon answered and said to Him, "Master, we have toiled all night and caught nothing; nevertheless at Your word I will let down the net." ⁶And when they had done this, they caught a great number of fish, and their net was breaking. ⁷So they signaled to their partners in the other boat to come and help them. And they came and filled both the boats, so that they began to sink. ⁸When Simon Peter saw it, he fell down at Jesus' knees, saying, "Depart from me, for I am a sinful man, O Lord!"

⁹For he and all who were with him were astonished at the catch of fish which they had taken; ¹⁰and so also were James and John, the sons of Zebedee, who were partners with Simon. And Jesus said to Simon, "Do not be afraid. From now on you will catch men."

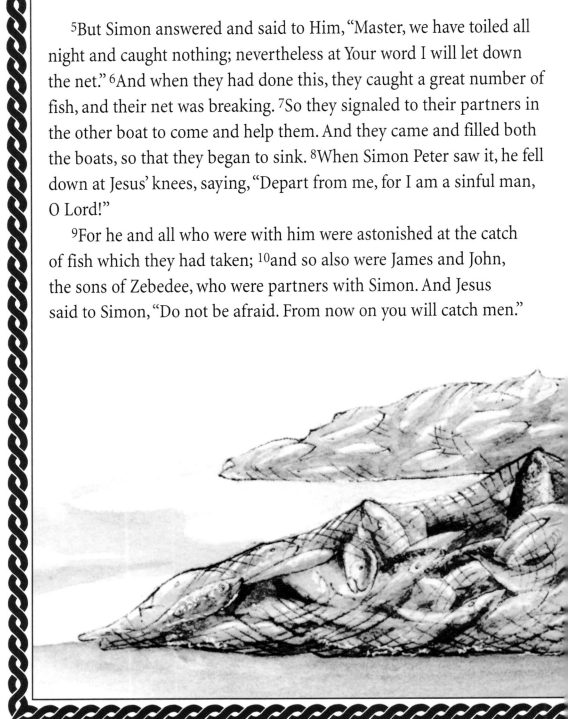

¹¹So when they had brought their boats to land, they forsook all and followed Him.

DISCOVER:
What did Jesus mean when he said to Simon that from then on they would "catch" men?

UNDERSTAND:
Jesus taught a lot of people as he sat in a boat on Lake Gennesaret. Then He told the fishermen to put down their nets, and they caught many fish.

LIVE IT OUT:
God says to us, "Follow me." We should say to God, "Lead me, and I will follow."

JESUS' FEET WASHED WITH TEARS

Luke 7:36–50

MEMORY VERSE:
And be kind to one another, tenderhearted, forgiving one another, even as God in Christ forgave you.

—*Ephesians 4:32*

7 ...³⁶Then one of the Pharisees asked Him to eat with him. And He went to the Pharisee's house, and sat down to eat. ³⁷And behold, a woman in the city who was a sinner, when she knew that Jesus sat at the table in the Pharisee's house, brought an alabaster flask of fragrant oil,

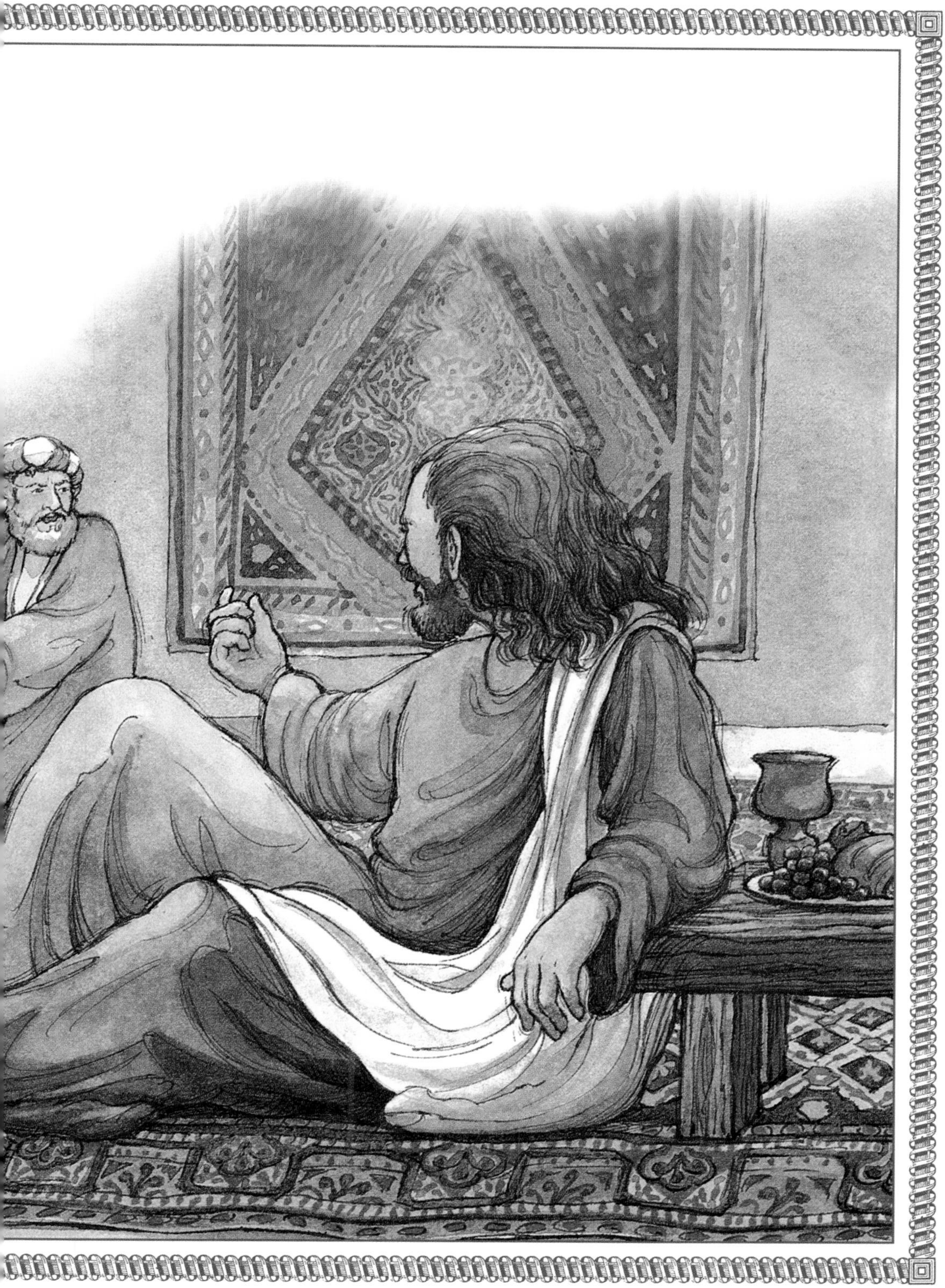

³⁸and stood at His feet behind Him weeping; and she began to wash His feet with her tears, and wiped them with the hair of her head; and she kissed His feet and anointed them with the fragrant oil. ³⁹Now when the Pharisee who had invited Him saw this, he spoke to himself, saying, "This Man, if He were a prophet, would know who and what manner of woman this is who is touching Him, for she is a sinner."

⁴⁰And Jesus answered and said to him, "Simon, I have something to say to you."

So he said, "Teacher, say it."

⁴¹"There was a certain creditor who had two debtors. One owed five hundred denarii, and the other fifty. ⁴²And when they had nothing with which to repay, he freely forgave them both. Tell Me, therefore, which of them will love him more?"

⁴³Simon answered and said, "I suppose the one whom he forgave more."

And He said to him, "You have rightly judged." ⁴⁴Then He turned to the woman and said to Simon, "Do you see this woman? I entered your house; you gave Me no water for My feet, but she has washed My feet with her tears and wiped them with the hair of her head. ⁴⁵You gave Me no kiss, but this woman has not ceased to kiss My feet since the time I came in. ⁴⁶You did not anoint My head with oil, but this woman has anointed My feet with fragrant oil. ⁴⁷Therefore I say to you, her sins, which are many, are forgiven, for she loved much. But to whom little is forgiven, the same loves little."

⁴⁸Then He said to her, "Your sins are forgiven."

⁴⁹And those who sat at the table with Him began to say to themselves, "Who is this who even forgives sins?"

⁵⁰Then He said to the woman, "Your faith has saved you. Go in peace."

DISCOVER:
How did the woman wash Jesus' feet? Did she show great love for Jesus?

UNDERSTAND:
Jesus knew the woman was a sinner. He accepted her anyway and forgave her sins.

LIVE IT OUT:
When we show our love for God and give ourselves to Him in faith, He forgives our sins.

THE GOOD SAMARITAN

Luke 10:30–37

MEMORY VERSE:
"Blessed are the merciful, for they shall obtain mercy."
—*Matthew 5:7*

10...³⁰Then Jesus answered and said: "A certain man went down from Jerusalem to Jericho, and fell among thieves, who stripped him of his clothing, wounded him, and departed, leaving him half dead. ³¹Now by chance a certain priest came down that road. And when he saw him, he passed by on the other side. ³²Likewise a Levite, when he arrived at the place, came and looked, and passed by on the other side. ³³But a certain Samaritan, as he journeyed, came where he was. And when he saw him, he had compassion. ³⁴So he went to him and bandaged his wounds, pouring on oil and wine; and he set him on his own animal, brought him to an inn, and took care of him. ³⁵On the next day, when he departed, he took out two denarii, gave them to the innkeeper, and said to him, 'Take care of him; and whatever more you spend, when I come again, I will repay you.' ³⁶So which of these three do you think was neighbor to him who fell among the thieves?"

³⁷And he said, "He who showed mercy on him."

Then Jesus said to him, "Go and do likewise."

DISCOVER:

Which one of the passersby showed compassion to the man who had been beaten?

UNDERSTAND:

The good man from Samaria put into practice the written law, which is to love God with all your heart, your soul, your strength, and your mind, and to love your neighbor as yourself.

LIVE IT OUT:

It's easy to look the other way when someone needs our help. But by helping those who are less fortunate than we are, we are following the message of God.

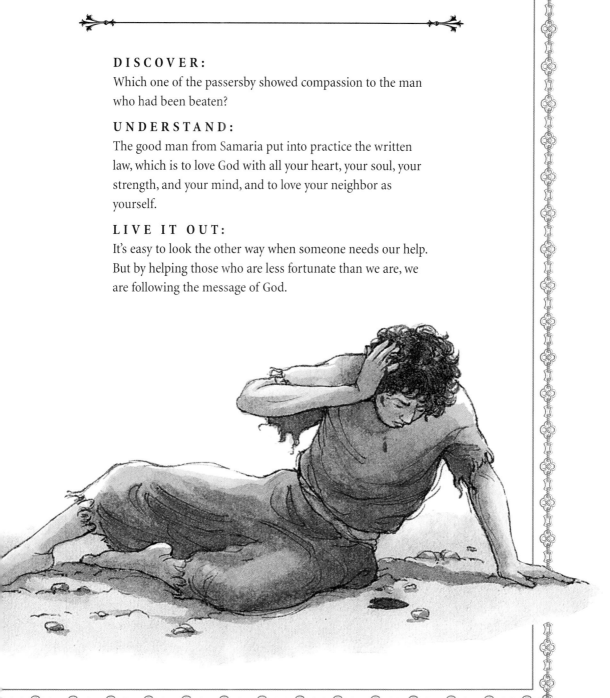

THE FORGIVING FATHER

Luke 15:11–24

MEMORY VERSE:
"For if you forgive men their trespasses, your heavenly Father will also forgive you."

—*Matthew 6:14*

15...¹¹Then He said: "A certain man had two sons. ¹²And the younger of them said to his father, 'Father, give me the portion of goods that falls to me.' So he divided to them his livelihood. ¹³And not many days after, the younger son gathered all together, journeyed to a far country, and there wasted his possessions with prodigal living. ¹⁴But when he had spent all, there arose a severe famine in that land, and he began to be in want. ¹⁵Then he went and joined himself to a citizen of that country, and he sent him into his fields to feed swine. ¹⁶And he would gladly have filled his stomach with the pods that the swine ate, and no one gave him anything.

¹⁷"But when he came to himself, he said, 'How many of my father's hired servants have bread enough and to spare, and I perish with hunger! ¹⁸I will arise and go to my father, and will say to him, "Father, I have sinned against heaven and before you, ¹⁹and I am no longer worthy to be called your son. Make me like one of your hired servants."'

²⁰"And he arose and came to his father. But when he was still a great way off, his father saw him and had compassion, and ran and fell on his neck and kissed him. ²¹And the son said to him, 'Father, I have sinned against heaven and in your sight, and am no longer worthy to be called your son.'

²²"But the father said to his servants, 'Bring out the best robe and put it on him, and put a ring on his hand and sandals on his feet. ²³And bring the fatted calf here and kill it, and let us eat and be merry; ²⁴for this my son was dead and is alive again; he was lost and is found.' And they began to be merry."

DISCOVER:
What did the younger son do with his portion of property from his father?

UNDERSTAND:
People call this story "The Prodigal Son." Prodigal means wasteful and careless. Even though the son was wasteful and careless, his father forgave him because his father loved him.

LIVE IT OUT:
Our Father in heaven loves us too. When we behave badly, He still wants us to return to Him. To go home, we just need to ask his forgiveness.

JESUS RISES TO HEAVEN

Luke 24:33–53

MEMORY VERSE:
And He said to them, "Go into all the world and preach the gospel to every creature."

—*Mark 16:15*

24… ³³So they rose up that very hour and returned to Jerusalem, and found the eleven and those who were with them gathered together, ³⁴saying, "The Lord is risen indeed, and has appeared to Simon!" ³⁵And they told about the things that had happened on the road, and how He was known to them in the breaking of bread.

³⁶Now as they said these things, Jesus Himself stood in the midst of them, and said to them, "Peace to you." ³⁷But they were terrified and frightened, and supposed they had seen a spirit. ³⁸And He said to them, "Why are you troubled? And why do doubts arise in your hearts? ³⁹Behold My hands and My feet, that it is I Myself. Handle Me and see, for a spirit does not have flesh and bones as you see I have."

⁴⁰When He had said this, He showed them His hands and His feet. ⁴¹But while they still did not believe for joy, and marveled, He said to them, "Have you any food here?" ⁴²So they gave Him a piece of a broiled fish and some honeycomb. ⁴³And He took it and ate in their presence.

⁴⁴Then He said to them, "These are the words which I spoke to you while I was still with you, that all things must be fulfilled which were written in the Law of Moses and the Prophets and the Psalms concerning Me." ⁴⁵And He opened their understanding, that they might comprehend the Scriptures.

⁴⁶Then He said to them, "Thus it is written, and thus it was necessary for the Christ to suffer and to rise from the dead the third day, ⁴⁷and that repentance and remission of sins should be preached in His name to all nations, beginning at Jerusalem. ⁴⁸And you are witnesses of these things. ⁴⁹Behold, I send the Promise of My Father upon you; but tarry in the city of Jerusalem until you are endued with power from on high."

⁵⁰And He led them out as far as Bethany, and He lifted up His hands and blessed them. ⁵¹Now it came to pass, while He blessed them, that He was parted from them and carried up into heaven. ⁵²And they worshiped Him, and returned to Jerusalem with great joy, ⁵³and were continually in the temple praising and blessing God. Amen.

DISCOVER:
What happened while Jesus was blessing His followers in Bethany?

UNDERSTAND:
Jesus said His disciples were witness to all that had happened to Him. Then He opened their minds so that they could understand the Scriptures, and told them to stay in Jerusalem until they received power from God.

LIVE IT OUT:
We praise the Lord for all He has done for us and tell others about Him in our daily lives.

A Blind Man Receives the Light

John 9:1–11, 30–33, 35–39

MEMORY VERSE:
Then Jesus spoke to them again, saying, "I am the light of the world. He who follows Me shall not walk in darkness, but have the light of life."

—John 8:12

9 Now as Jesus passed by, He saw a man who was blind from birth. ²And His disciples asked Him, saying, "Rabbi, who sinned, this man or his parents, that he was born blind?"

³Jesus answered, "Neither this man nor his parents sinned, but that the works of God should be revealed in him. ⁴I must work the works of Him who sent Me while it is day; the night is coming when no one can work. ⁵As long as I am in the world, I am the light of the world."

⁶When He had said these things, He spat on the ground and made clay with the saliva; and He anointed the eyes of the blind man with the clay. ⁷And He said to him, "Go, wash in the pool of Siloam" (which is translated, Sent). So he went and washed, and came back seeing. ⁸Therefore the neighbors and those who previously had seen that he was blind said, "Is not this he who sat and begged?"

⁹Some said, "This is he." Others said, "He is like him."

He said, "I am he."

¹⁰Therefore they said to him, "How were your eyes opened?"

¹¹He answered and said, "A Man called Jesus made clay and anointed my eyes and said to me, 'Go to the pool of Siloam and wash.' So I went and washed, and I received sight." . . .

They brought the man to the Pharisees. The man again told how Jesus had given him sight, and again he answered many questions. Some believed Jesus was not from God, others believed Jesus was from God. But none knew where "this fellow" Jesus was from.

³⁰The man answered and said to them, "Why, this is a marvelous thing, that you do not know where He is from; yet He has opened my eyes! ³¹Now we know that God does not hear sinners; but if anyone is a worshiper of God and does His will, He hears him. ³²Since the world began it has been unheard of that anyone opened the eyes of one who was born blind. ³³If this Man were not from God, He could do nothing." . . .

But they did not believe the man and threw him out.

35Jesus heard that they had cast him out; and when He had found him, He said to him, "Do you believe in the Son of God?"

36He answered and said, "Who is He, Lord, that I may believe in Him?"

37And Jesus said to him, "You have both seen Him and it is He who is talking with you."

38Then he said, "Lord, I believe!" And he worshiped Him.

39And Jesus said, "For judgment I have come into this world, that those who do not see may see, and that those who see may be made blind."

DISCOVER:
How did the people question each other about the blind man's sight? How did they question the blind man about his sight being restored?

UNDERSTAND:
No one believed the blind man's explanation about how Jesus made him see. What did Jesus say about this?

LIVE IT OUT:
Let the light of the Lord shine through in your life.

LAZARUS IS RAISED FROM THE DEAD

John 11:1, 3–5, 25–27, 32, 40–44

MEMORY VERSE:
For of Him and through Him and to Him are all things, to
whom be glory forever. Amen.

—*Romans 11:36*

11 Now a certain man was sick, Lazarus of Bethany, the town of
Mary and her sister Martha. . . . ³Therefore the sisters sent to Him,
saying, "Lord, behold, he whom You love is sick."

⁴When Jesus heard that, He said, "This sickness is not unto death,
but for the glory of God, that the Son of God may be glorified
through it."

⁵Now Jesus loved Martha and her sister and Lazarus. . . .

When Jesus heard Lazarus was sick, He and His disciples went to
see Lazarus. By the time they arrived, Lazarus had been dead four days
and his body had been placed in a cave with a large stone covering the
opening. But Jesus told Martha that Lazarus would rise again.

²⁵Jesus said to her, "I am the resurrection and the life. He who
believes in Me, though he may die, he shall live. ²⁶And whoever lives
and believes in Me shall never die. Do you believe this?"

²⁷She said to Him, "Yes, Lord, I believe that You are the Christ, the
Son of God, who is to come into the world." . . .

Martha went to Mary and told her the Teacher wanted to see her. Mary, and the Jews who were comforting her, went to where Jesus was staying.

32Then, when Mary came where Jesus was, and saw Him, she fell down at His feet, saying to Him, "Lord, if You had been here, my brother would not have died." . . .

When Jesus saw Mary weeping, He asked her to take Him to Lazarus' tomb. And Jesus wept, too. When they reached the tomb, Jesus told those around him to take away the stone, but Martha protested, saying that by this time there would be a strong smell.

⁴⁰Jesus said to her *[Martha]*, "Did I not say to you that if you would believe you would see the glory of God?" ⁴¹Then they took away the stone from the place where the dead man was lying. And Jesus lifted up His eyes and said, "Father, I thank You that You have heard Me. ⁴²And I know that You always hear Me, but because of the people who are standing by I said this, that they may believe that You sent Me." ⁴³Now when He had said these things, He cried with a loud voice, "Lazarus, come forth!" ⁴⁴And he who had died came out bound hand and foot with graveclothes, and his face was wrapped with a cloth. Jesus said to them, "Loose him, and let him go."

DISCOVER:
How long had Lazarus been dead when Jesus arrived in Bethany? What did Martha, Lazarus's sister, say to Jesus?

UNDERSTAND:
Martha believed in the power of the Lord. Her faith was rewarded when Lazarus, her brother, was raised from the dead.

LIVE IT OUT:
Jesus promises everlasting life to all who believe in Him.

Jesus Serves the Disciples

John 13:1–17

MEMORY VERSE:
"And whoever desires to be first among you, let him be your slave—just as the Son of Man did not come to be served, but to serve, and to give His life a ransom for many."

—*Matthew 20:27–28*

13 Now before the Feast of the Passover, when Jesus knew that His hour had come that He should depart from this world to the Father, having loved His own who were in the world, He loved them to the end.

2And supper being ended, the devil having already put it into the heart of Judas Iscariot, Simon's son, to betray Him, 3Jesus, knowing that the Father had given all things into His hands, and that He had come from God and was going to God, 4rose from supper and laid aside His garments, took a towel and girded Himself. 5After that, He poured water into a basin and began to wash the disciples' feet, and to wipe them with the towel with which He was girded. 6Then He came to Simon Peter. And Peter said to Him, "Lord, are You washing my feet?"

7Jesus answered and said to him, "What I am doing you do not understand now, but you will know after this."

8Peter said to Him, "You shall never wash my feet!"

Jesus answered him, "If I do not wash you, you have no part with Me."

⁹Simon Peter said to Him, "Lord, not my feet only, but also my hands and my head!"

¹⁰Jesus said to him, "He who is bathed needs only to wash his feet, but is completely clean; and you are clean, but not all of you." ¹¹For He knew who would betray Him; therefore He said, "You are not all clean."

¹²So when He had washed their feet, taken His garments, and sat down again, He said to them, "Do you know what I have done to you?

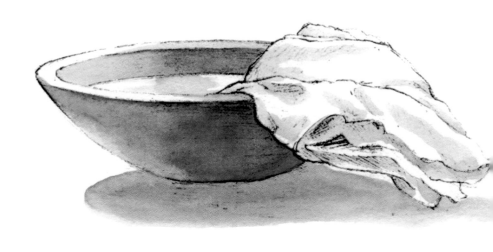

13You call Me Teacher and Lord, and you say well, for so I am. 14If I then, your Lord and Teacher, have washed your feet, you also ought to wash one another's feet. 15For I have given you an example, that you should do as I have done to you. 16Most assuredly, I say to you, a servant is not greater than his master; nor is he who is sent greater than he who sent him. 17If you know these things, blessed are you if you do them." . . .

DISCOVER:
Who put it in the heart of Judas Iscariot to betray Jesus?

UNDERSTAND:
By washing the disciples' feet, Jesus was demonstrating the need to serve others.

LIVE IT OUT:
We show our love for God when we serve others with a joyful heart.

Disciples Find the Tomb Empty

John 20:1–10

20 Now the first day of the week Mary Magdalene went to the tomb early, while it was still dark, and saw that the stone had been taken away from the tomb. ²Then she ran and came to Simon Peter, and to the other disciple, whom Jesus loved, and said to them, "They have taken away the Lord out of the tomb, and we do not know where they have laid Him."

³Peter therefore went out, and the other disciple, and were going to the tomb. ⁴So they both ran together, and the other disciple outran Peter and came to the tomb first. ⁵And he, stooping down and looking in, saw the linen cloths lying there; yet he did not go in. ⁶Then Simon Peter came, following him, and went into the tomb; and he saw the linen cloths lying there, ⁷and the handkerchief that had been around His head, not lying with the linen cloths, but folded together in a place by itself. ⁸Then the other disciple, who came to the tomb first, went in also; and he saw and believed. ⁹For as yet they did not know the Scripture, that He must rise again from the dead. ¹⁰Then the disciples went away again to their own homes.

DISCOVER:

What did Mary Magdalene see when she went to the tomb before daylight?

UNDERSTAND:

When the disciples found the tomb empty, they did not know what had happened to Jesus, because they did not have the "rest of the story" as we do today.

LIVE IT OUT:

Like Mary Magdalene, tell others what you learn about Jesus.

Philip and the Eunuch

Acts 8:26–40

MEMORY VERSE:
"He who believes and is baptized will be saved; but he who does not believe will be condemned."

—*Mark 16:16*

8...²⁶Now an angel of the Lord spoke to Philip, saying, "Arise and go toward the south along the road which goes down from Jerusalem to Gaza." This is desert. ²⁷So he arose and went. And behold, a man of Ethiopia, a eunuch of great authority under Candace the queen of the Ethiopians, who had charge of all her treasury, and had come to Jerusalem to worship, ²⁸was returning. And sitting in his chariot, he was reading Isaiah the prophet. ²⁹Then the Spirit said to Philip, "Go near and overtake this chariot."

³⁰So Philip ran to him, and heard him reading the prophet Isaiah, and said, "Do you understand what you are reading?"

³¹And he said, "How can I, unless someone guides me?" And he asked Philip to come up and sit with him. ³²The place in the Scripture which he read was this:

"He was led as a sheep to the slaughter; and as a lamb before its shearer is silent, so He opened not His mouth. 33In His humiliation His justice was taken away, and who will declare His generation? For His life is taken from the earth."

34So the eunuch answered Philip and said, "I ask you, of whom does the prophet say this, of himself or of some other man?" 35Then Philip opened his mouth, and beginning at this Scripture, preached Jesus to him. 36Now as they went down the road, they came to some water. And the eunuch said, "See, here is water. What hinders me from being baptized?"

37Then Philip said, "If you believe with all your heart, you may."

And he answered and said, "I believe that Jesus Christ is the Son of God."

³⁸So he commanded the chariot to stand still. And both Philip and the eunuch went down into the water, and he baptized him. ³⁹Now when they came up out of the water, the Spirit of the Lord caught Philip away, so that the eunuch saw him no more; and he went on his way rejoicing. ⁴⁰But Philip was found at Azotus. And passing through, he preached in all the cities till he came to Caesarea.

DISCOVER:

What was Philip doing when he met the Ethiopian eunuch? How did he know about the eunuch?

UNDERSTAND:

As Philip and the eunuch traveled down the road, Philip was preaching about Jesus to him. The eunuch became a believer and was baptized.

LIVE IT OUT:

We should believe with all our heart that Jesus Christ is the Son of God.

SAUL ON THE ROAD TO DAMASCUS

Acts 9:3–18

MEMORY VERSE:
And I thank Christ Jesus our Lord who has enabled me, because He counted me faithful, putting me into the ministry, although I was formerly a blasphemer, a persecutor, and an insolent man; but I obtained mercy because I did it ignorantly in unbelief.

—*1 Timothy 1:12–13*

9 ...³As he *[Saul]* journeyed he came near Damascus, and suddenly a light shone around him from heaven. ⁴Then he fell to the ground, and heard a voice saying to him, "Saul, Saul, why are you persecuting Me?"

⁵And he said, "Who are You, Lord?"

Then the Lord said, "I am Jesus, whom you are persecuting. It is hard for you to kick against the goads."

⁶So he, trembling and astonished, said, "Lord, what do You want me to do?"

Then the Lord said to him, "Arise and go into the city, and you will be told what you must do."

⁷And the men who journeyed with him stood speechless, hearing a voice but seeing no one. ⁸Then Saul arose from the ground, and when his eyes were opened he saw no one. But they led him by the hand and brought him

into Damascus. ⁹And he was three days without sight, and neither ate nor drank.

¹⁰Now there was a certain disciple at Damascus named Ananias; and to him the Lord said in a vision, "Ananias."

And he said, "Here I am, Lord."

¹¹So the Lord said to him, "Arise and go to the street called Straight, and inquire at the house of Judas for one called Saul of Tarsus, for behold, he is praying. ¹²And in a vision he has seen a man named Ananias coming in and putting his hand on him, so that he might receive his sight."

¹³Then Ananias answered, "Lord, I have heard from many about this man, how much harm he has done to Your saints in Jerusalem.

¹⁴And here he has authority from the chief priests to bind all who call on Your name."

¹⁵But the Lord said to him, "Go, for he is a chosen vessel of Mine to bear My name before Gentiles, kings, and the children of Israel. ¹⁶For I will show him how many things he must suffer for My name's sake."

¹⁷And Ananias went his way and entered the house; and laying his hands on him he said, "Brother Saul, the Lord Jesus, who appeared to you on the road as you came, has sent me that you may receive your sight and be filled with the Holy Spirit." ¹⁸Immediately there fell from his eyes something like scales, and he received his sight at once; and he arose and was baptized.

DISCOVER:
What did Ananias say to Saul when he arrived at the house of Judas of Damascus?

UNDERSTAND:
On the way to Damascus, the Lord caused Saul to be blinded because of his hatred of Christians. Then the Lord spoke to Ananias in a dream and sent him to the house of Judas of Damascus, where Saul was staying. When Ananias touched Saul, Saul's sight was restored, and he too became a follower of Jesus.

LIVE IT OUT:
We must wait patiently for the Lord to guide us, and we must be willing to listen and learn.

SAUL ESCAPES IN A BASKET

Acts 9:23–25

MEMORY VERSE:
Our God is the God of salvation; and to GOD the Lord belong escapes from death.

—Psalm 68:20

9...²³Now after many days were past, the Jews plotted to kill him *[Saul]*. ²⁴But their plot became known to Saul. And they watched the gates day and night, to kill him. ²⁵Then the disciples took him by night and let him down through the wall in a large basket.

DISCOVER:
How was Saul saved from the Jews?

UNDERSTAND:
Some people were angry with Saul and did not believe what he taught. They wanted to kill him.

LIVE IT OUT:
When you pray, ask God, "What do you want me to do?"

An Angel Frees Peter

Acts 12:5–16

12...⁵Peter was therefore kept in prison, but constant prayer was offered to God for him by the church. ⁶And when Herod was about to bring him out, that night Peter was sleeping, bound with two chains between two soldiers; and the guards before the door were keeping the prison. ⁷Now behold, an angel of the Lord stood by him, and a light shone in the prison; and he struck Peter on the side and raised him up, saying, "Arise quickly!" And his chains fell off his hands. ⁸Then the angel said to him, "Gird yourself and tie on your sandals"; and so he did. And he said to him, "Put on your garment and follow me." ⁹So he went out and followed him, and did not know that what was done by the angel was real, but thought he was seeing a vision. ¹⁰When they were past the first and the second guard posts, they came to the iron gate that leads to the city, which opened to them of its own accord; and they went out and went down one street, and immediately the angel departed from him.

¹¹And when Peter had come to himself, he said, "Now I know for certain that the Lord has sent His angel, and has delivered me from the hand of Herod and from all the expectation of the Jewish people."

¹²So, when he had considered this, he came to the house of Mary, the mother of John whose surname was Mark, where many were gathered together praying. ¹³And as Peter knocked at the door of the gate, a girl named Rhoda came to answer. ¹⁴When she recognized Peter's voice, because of her gladness she did not open the gate, but ran in and announced that Peter stood before the gate. ¹⁵But they said to her, "You are beside yourself!" Yet she kept insisting that it was so. So they said, "It is his angel."

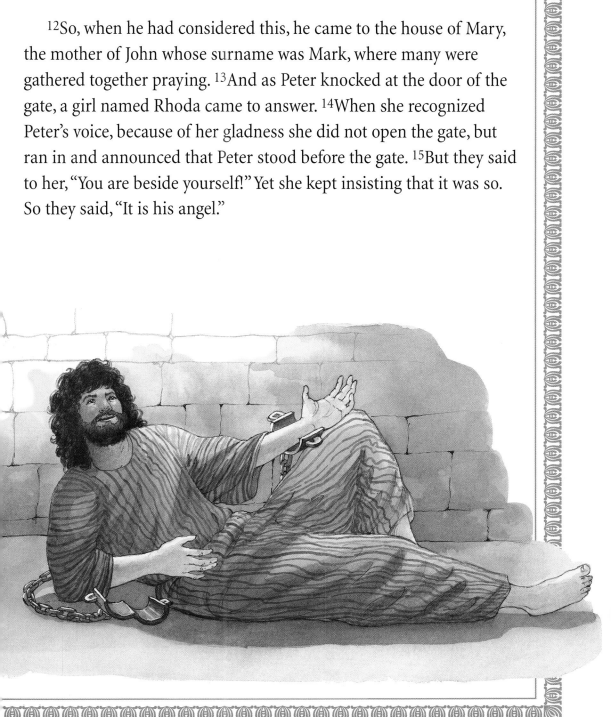

¹⁶Now Peter continued knocking; and when they opened the door and saw him, they were astonished.

DISCOVER:

Did Peter think he was dreaming when the angel of God freed him from prison?

UNDERSTAND:

The church members constantly prayed for Peter when he was in prison. Yet they were astonished when Peter appeared at the gate.

LIVE IT OUT:

Pray for God's angels to watch over us as they watched over Peter.

The First Missionaries

Acts 14:8–19

MEMORY VERSE:
"Go therefore and make disciples of all the nations, baptizing them in the name of the Father and of the Son and of the Holy Spirit, teaching them to observe all things that I have commanded you; and lo, I am with you always, even to the end of the age." Amen.

—*Matthew 28:19-20*

Barnabas was a good man, full of the Holy Spirit and of faith. Barnabas and Paul, also known as Saul, went to Antioch, where men were preaching about Jesus. Together Barnabas and Paul taught a great many people. And the disciples were first called Christians in Antioch.

Barnabas and Saul then left Antioch and traveled the region, bringing people to God. They are considered by some to be the first missionaries.

14...⁸And in Lystra a certain man without strength in his feet was sitting, a cripple from his mother's womb, who had never walked. ⁹This man heard Paul speaking. Paul, observing him intently and seeing that he had faith to be healed, ¹⁰said with a loud voice, "Stand up straight on your feet!" And he leaped and walked. ¹¹Now when the people saw what Paul had done, they raised their voices, saying in the Lycaonian language, "The gods have come down to us in the likeness of men!" 12And Barnabas they called Zeus, and Paul, Hermes, because he was the chief speaker. 13Then the priest of Zeus, whose temple was in front of their city, brought oxen and garlands to the gates, intending to sacrifice with the multitudes.

14But when the apostles Barnabas and Paul heard this, they tore their clothes and ran in among the multitude, crying out 15and saying, "Men, why are you doing these things? We also are men with the same nature as you, and preach to you that you should turn from these useless things to the living God, who made the heaven, the earth, the sea, and all things that are in them, 16who in bygone generations allowed all nations to walk in their own ways.

¹⁷Nevertheless
He did not leave
Himself without witness,
in that He did good, gave us rain
from heaven and fruitful seasons, filling our hearts with food and
gladness." ¹⁸And with these sayings they could scarcely restrain the
multitudes from sacrificing to them.

¹⁹Then Jews from Antioch and Iconium came there; and having
persuaded the multitudes, they stoned Paul and dragged him out of
the city, supposing him to be dead. . . .

*However, when the disciples gathered around him, Paul rose up and went
into the city. And so Barnabas and Paul went from city to city and preached
the gospel.*

DISCOVER:
In what city were the disciples first called Christians? What
were the goals of Paul and Barnabas?

UNDERSTAND:
Barnabas was a good man, full of the Holy Spirit and of
faith. A great number of people turned to the Lord because
of Barnabas.

LIVE IT OUT:
As Christians we are models of God's work on earth. We
should live our lives as good models, so we bring others to
God by our example.

GOD OPENS LYDIA'S HEART

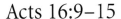

Acts 16:9–15

MEMORY VERSE:
Then I will give them a heart to know Me, that I am the
LORD; and they shall be My people, and I will be their God,
for they shall return to Me with their whole heart.

—*Jeremiah 24:7*

16...⁹And a vision appeared to Paul in the night. A man of
Macedonia stood and pleaded with him, saying, "Come over to
Macedonia and help us." ¹⁰Now after he had seen the vision,
immediately we sought to go to Macedonia, concluding that the
Lord had called us to preach the gospel to them.

¹¹Therefore, sailing from Troas, we ran a straight course to
Samothrace, and the next day came to Neapolis, ¹²and from there
to Philippi, which is the foremost city of that part of Macedonia,
a colony. And we were staying in that city for some days. ¹³And
on the Sabbath day we went out of the city to the riverside,
where prayer was customarily made; and we sat down and

spoke to the women who met there. [14]Now a certain woman named Lydia heard us. She was a seller of purple from the city of Thyatira, who worshiped God. The Lord opened her heart to heed the things spoken by Paul. [15]And when she and her household were baptized, she begged us, saying, "If you have judged me to be faithful to the Lord, come to my house and stay." So she persuaded us.

DISCOVER:

What were the women doing at the river when Paul spoke to them? Did Lydia listen to Paul?

UNDERSTAND:

Lydia and the people who lived in her house were the first people in Europe to become Christians.

LIVE IT OUT:

Ask God to give you an open heart so that you may know when He speaks to you.

SHIPWRECKED!

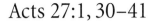

Acts 27:1, 30–41

MEMORY VERSE:
But the wicked are like the troubled sea, when it cannot
rest, whose waters cast up mire and dirt.

—*Isaiah 57:20*

27 And when it was decided that we should sail to Italy, they
delivered Paul and some other prisoners to one named Julius, a
centurion of the Augustan Regiment....

³⁰And as the sailors were seeking to escape from the ship, when
they had let down the skiff into the sea, under pretense of putting out
anchors from the prow, ³¹Paul said to the centurion and the soldiers,
"Unless these men stay in the ship, you cannot be saved." ³²Then the
soldiers cut away the ropes of the skiff and let it fall off.

³³And as day was about to dawn, Paul implored them all to take
food, saying, "Today is the fourteenth day you have waited and
continued without food, and eaten nothing. ³⁴Therefore I urge you to
take nourishment, for this is for your survival, since not a hair will fall
from the head of any of you." ³⁵And when he had said these things, he
took bread and gave thanks to God in the presence of them all; and
when he had broken it he began to eat. ³⁶Then they were all encouraged,
and also took food themselves. ³⁷And in all we were two hundred and

seventy-six persons on the ship. ³⁸So when they had eaten enough, they lightened the ship and threw out the wheat into the sea.

³⁹When it was day, they did not recognize the land; but they observed a bay with a beach, onto which they planned to run the ship if possible. ⁴⁰And they let go the anchors and left them in the sea, meanwhile

loosing the rudder ropes; and they hoisted the mainsail to the wind and made for shore. ⁴¹But striking a place where two seas met, they ran the ship aground; and the prow stuck fast and remained immovable, but the stern was being broken up by the violence of the waves.

DISCOVER:

Was Paul a great help before the shipwreck? After the sailors had eaten, what did they do with the wheat?

UNDERSTAND:

Paul urged the men to take heart because an angel had told him no one on the ship would die.

LIVE IT OUT:

We are not alone in the world, for God is always with us.

GOD'S POWER

---

2 Corinthians 4:7–15

MEMORY VERSE:

And He said to me, "My grace is sufficient for you, for My strength is made perfect in weakness." Therefore most gladly I will rather boast in my infirmities, that the power of Christ may rest upon me.

—2 Corinthians 12:9

4...⁷But we have this treasure in earthen vessels, that the excellence of the power may be of God and not of us. ⁸We are hard-pressed on every side, yet not crushed; we are perplexed, but not in despair; ⁹persecuted, but not forsaken; struck down, but not destroyed—¹⁰always carrying about in the body the dying of the Lord Jesus, that the life of Jesus also may be manifested in our body. ¹¹For we who live are always

delivered to death for Jesus' sake, that the life of Jesus also may be manifested in our mortal flesh. ¹²So then death is working in us, but life in you.

¹³And since we have the same spirit of faith, according to what is written, "I believed and therefore I spoke," we also believe and therefore speak, ¹⁴knowing that He who raised up the Lord Jesus will also raise us up with Jesus, and will present us with you. ¹⁵For all things are for your sakes, that grace, having spread through the many, may cause thanksgiving to abound to the glory of God.

DISCOVER:

What effect will grace have when it is spread through many people?

UNDERSTAND:

Paul said to not lose heart because the love and thanks of many will bring glory to God.

LIVE IT OUT:

Don't lose heart when times are bad, for God is with us and He will help us.

GOD'S ARMOR

Ephesians 6:10–20

MEMORY VERSE:
Put on the whole armor of God, that you may be able to
stand against the wiles of the devil.

—Ephesians 6:11

6...¹⁰𝔉inally, my brethren, be strong in the Lord and in the power of His might. ¹¹Put on the whole armor of God, that you may be able to stand against the wiles of the devil. ¹²For we do not wrestle against flesh and blood, but against principalities, against powers, against the rulers of the darkness of this age, against spiritual hosts of wickedness in the heavenly places. ¹³Therefore take up the whole armor of God, that you may be able to withstand in the evil day, and having done all, to stand.

¹⁴Stand therefore, having girded your waist with truth, having put on the breastplate of righteousness, ¹⁵and having shod your feet with the preparation of the gospel of peace; ¹⁶above all, taking the shield of faith with which you will be able to quench all the fiery darts of the wicked one. ¹⁷And take the helmet of salvation, and the sword of the Spirit, which is the word of God; ¹⁸praying always with all prayer and supplication in the Spirit, being watchful to this end with all perseverance and

supplication for all the saints—¹⁹and for me, that utterance may be given to me, that I may open my mouth boldly to make known the mystery of the gospel, ²⁰for which I am an ambassador in chains; that in it I may speak boldly, as I ought to speak.

DISCOVER:
What did Paul want the Christians at Ephesus to do? Why?

UNDERSTAND:
The armor of God is not armor like a knight would wear. It is the strength we have as believers to do the right thing. Paul's letter to the church at Ephesus urges them to be strong in the Lord, and above all to have faith.

LIVE IT OUT:
When we study the Bible, pray, speak the truth, and have faith, it keeps us strong for the Lord.

CHRIST COMES BACK!

1 Thessalonians 4:13—5:1

MEMORY VERSE:
And if I go and prepare a place for you, I will come again
and receive you to Myself; that where I am, there you may
be also.

—John 14:3

4 …¹³But I do not want you to be ignorant, brethren, concerning those who have fallen asleep, lest you sorrow as others who have no hope. ¹⁴For if we believe that Jesus died and rose again, even so God will bring with Him those who sleep in Jesus.

¹⁵For this we say to you by the word of the Lord, that we who are alive and remain until the coming of the Lord will by no means precede those who are asleep. ¹⁶For the Lord Himself will descend from heaven with a shout, with the voice of an archangel, and with the trumpet of God. And the dead in Christ will rise first. ¹⁷Then we who are alive and remain shall be caught up together with them in the clouds to meet the Lord in the air. And thus we shall always be with the Lord. ¹⁸Therefore comfort one another with these words.

5 But concerning the times and the seasons, brethren, you have no need that I should write to you.

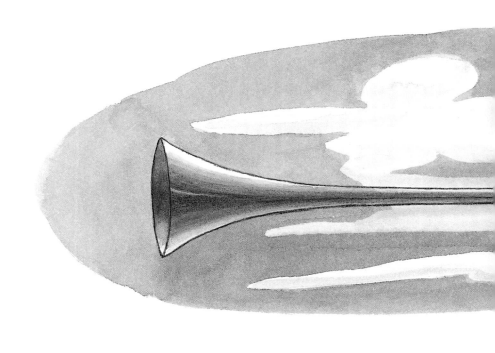

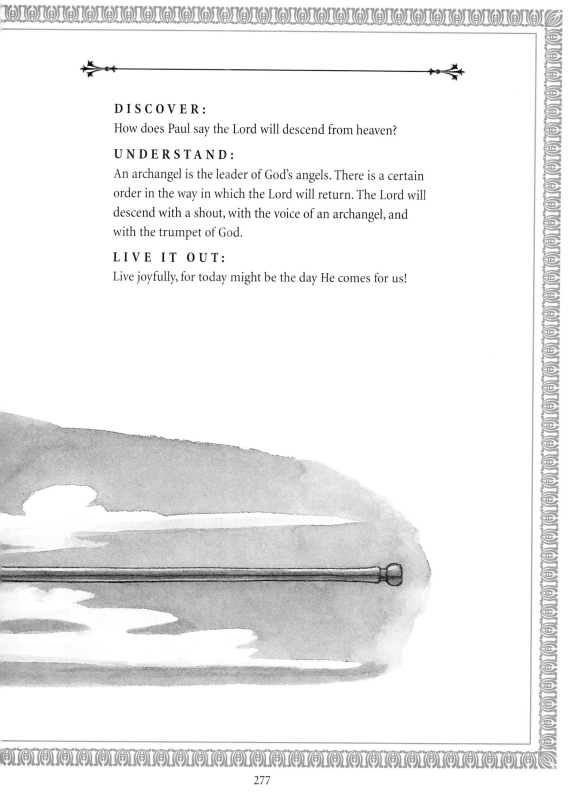

DISCOVER:

How does Paul say the Lord will descend from heaven?

UNDERSTAND:

An archangel is the leader of God's angels. There is a certain order in the way in which the Lord will return. The Lord will descend with a shout, with the voice of an archangel, and with the trumpet of God.

LIVE IT OUT:

Live joyfully, for today might be the day He comes for us!

HEAVEN IS OPENED

Hebrews 12:22–29

MEMORY VERSE:

Now I saw a new heaven and a new earth, for the first heaven and the first earth had passed away. Also there was no more sea.

—Revelation 21:1

12...²²But you have come to Mount Zion and to the city of the living God, the heavenly Jerusalem, to an innumerable company of angels, ²³to the general assembly and church of the firstborn who are registered in heaven, to God the Judge of all, to the spirits of just men made perfect, ²⁴to Jesus the Mediator of the new covenant, and to the blood of sprinkling that speaks better things than that of Abel.

²⁵See that you do not refuse Him who speaks. For if they did not escape who refused Him who spoke on earth, much more shall we not escape if we turn away from Him who speaks from heaven, ²⁶whose voice then shook the earth; but now He has promised, saying, "Yet once more I shake not only the earth, but also heaven." ²⁷Now this, "Yet once more," indicates the removal of those things that are being shaken, as of things that are made, that the things which cannot be shaken may remain.

²⁸Therefore, since we are receiving a kingdom which cannot be shaken, let us have grace, by which we may serve God acceptably with reverence and godly fear. ²⁹For our God is a consuming fire.

DISCOVER:
Who is speaking to the Hebrews in verse 26?

UNDERSTAND:
Part of God's grace is His forgiveness for the wrong things we do. He has shown us kindness and love, even though we don't deserve them.

LIVE IT OUT:
Let us have grace so that we may serve God in a way that pleases Him.

KNOWING GOD'S LOVE

1 John 4:7–11

MEMORY VERSE:
And this commandment we have from Him: that he who loves God must love his brother also.

—1 John 4:21

4...⁷Beloved, let us love one another, for love is of God; and everyone who loves is born of God and knows God. ⁸He who does not love does not know God, for God is love. ⁹In this the love of God was manifested toward us, that God has sent His only begotten Son into the world, that we might live through Him. ¹⁰In this is love, not that we loved God, but that He loved us and sent His Son to be the propitiation for our sins. ¹¹Beloved, if God so loved us, we also ought to love one another.

DISCOVER:
Is it possible to know God if we don't love one another?

UNDERSTAND:
God loved us so much He sent His only Son, Jesus, to save us. God expects us to love others the way He loves us.

LIVE IT OUT:
Sometimes it's hard to love others, but ask God to help you. We must love one another, putting others' needs before our own.

People from Every Tribe and Nation

Revelation 7:9–17

MEMORY VERSE:
And all flesh shall see the salvation of God.

—Luke 3:6

7 ...9After these things I looked, and behold, a great multitude which no one could number, of all nations, tribes, peoples, and tongues, standing before the throne and before the Lamb, clothed with white robes, with palm branches in their hands, 10and crying out with a loud voice, saying, "Salvation belongs to our God who sits on the throne, and to the Lamb!" 11All the angels stood around the throne and the elders and the four living creatures, and fell on their faces before the throne and worshiped God, 12saying:

"Amen! Blessing and glory and wisdom, thanksgiving and honor and power and might, be to our God forever and ever. Amen."

13Then one of the elders answered, saying to me, "Who are these arrayed in white robes, and where did they come from?"

14And I said to him, "Sir, you know."

So he said to me, "These are the ones who come out of the great tribulation, and washed their robes and made them white in the blood of the Lamb. 15Therefore they are before the throne of God, and serve

Him day and night in His temple. And He who sits on the throne will dwell among them. ¹⁶They shall neither hunger anymore nor thirst anymore; the sun shall not strike them, nor any heat; ¹⁷for the Lamb who is in the midst of the throne will shepherd them and lead them to living fountains of waters. And God will wipe away every tear from their eyes."

DISCOVER:
What did the angels around the throne do? What did they say?

UNDERSTAND:
In heaven John saw Christ standing before all nations, tribes, peoples, and languages. This is because God's heart reaches out to the whole world, offering peace and love.

LIVE IT OUT:
As believers we should be vocal in giving God the glory, thanks, and honor for our salvation, not only because it belongs to Him, but so others may find Him, too.

GLOSSARY

alabaster. A white, fine-grained gypsum used to make beautiful containers. Perfume or oils were often kept in alabaster containers.

archangel. The title given to Michael, the leader of God's angels.

armorbearer. A male who carries the protective covering and/or weapons for a warrior.

balm. An ointment or lotion that is often made from plants or trees for medical uses. It was often used to heal sore skin.

barren. Incapable of reproducing. A woman who cannot have children is sometimes called a barren woman. A land that cannot grow plants is called barren land.

basin. A sink or bowl used for washing. It's usually not very deep.

betray. To break a trust.

birthright. A right someone is given because of the order in which he was born into a certain family, nation, or culture. In biblical times, the birthright was usually given to the firstborn son.

boisterous. Noisy, loud, out of control; lively.

bronze fetters. A type of restraint. These were made of the alloy bronze and were shackles or chains for the feet.

chariot. A two-wheeled cart for one person, generally pulled by two or more horses. Usually driven standing up. It was used in battles, traveling, races, and ceremonies like parades.

clean animal. Any animal that both chewed the cud (the food returning from the first stomach to the mouth to be chewed a second time) and had a cleft (split) hoof, and could therefore be eaten. A cow is a clean animal that chews the cud and has a cleft hoof *(see unclean animal).*

countenance. The look or expression on a person's face; sometimes described as a calm, controlled look.

covenant. A contract or promise.

cubit. An ancient unit of measure originally the length of the forearm, from elbow to the tip of the middle finger (about 17 to 22 inches).

denarii. The plural of denarius. A silver coin of ancient Rome. Roman soldiers worked for one denarius a day.

descendant. A person who is born to a person or to their children. This includes grandchildren, great-grandchildren, and so forth.

dwelling. A home or shelter.

Egyptian. A native of Egypt, a country in the northeast part of Africa that was an ancient kingdom.

ephah. A dry measurement. One ephah is 10 omers. It is equal to three-fifths of a bushel or 22 liters.

eunuch. A man who cannot father children. Eunuchs were often placed in positions of trust and authority.

flask. A container. A flask can be a large container like a pitcher, or a small container like a perfume bottle.

forsaken. Left, abandoned, or given up.

frankincense. A very sweet-smelling perfume made from a gum resin found in Arabian and northeast African trees, called Boswellia trees. It was often used in medical and fumigating preparations, and is still used as incense.

fugitive. A person who is running away, especially from the law.

gaunt. Extremely thin and bony from great hunger. In Pharaoh's dream he saw seven fat cows and seven gaunt cows.

genealogy. A person's family history, usually in a chart form, that shows the person's relatives, which can go all the way back to their first ancestors.

gird. To encircle or bind with a belt or band.

glean. To follow the harvesters and gather what grain or fruit is left. In biblical times, what was left in the fields by the first harvesters was for the poor to gather.

goad. A sharp pointed metal rod used to prod animals and/or used as a dangerous weapon; to tease or encourage someone to do something.

gopherwood. The type of wood God commanded Noah to use to build the ark. Some think that it is what we know today as cypress wood.

graveclothes. The clothes someone is buried in, or the wrappings used around the body of someone to be buried.

iniquity. A wicked act or sin.

interpreter. A person who speaks more than one language and can translate a message between speakers who speak different languages.

Ishmaelite. A descendant of Ishmael, the traditional ancestor of the Arab peoples *(see descendant)*.

javelin. A light spear thrown by hand.

lame. Physically disabled. Usually limping or having difficulty walking. It can also mean weak.

leprosy. A contagious disease that attacks the skin, flesh, and nerves. Often people with leprosy (sometimes called lepers) have scaly scabs on their skin, must have

limbs amputated, and their bodies look shriveled and weak. In biblical times, people didn't know leprosy was caused by a bacterium. They didn't have any medical treatment or understanding of the disease or how to avoid catching it; therefore, lepers were forced to live outside the cities and warn people of their condition by yelling "Unclean! Unclean!"

linger. To stay in one place longer than expected.

mainsail. A sail on water vessels like boats and ships. It is a large piece of canvas or other fabric that uses the force of wind as the energy to drive and steer the vessel.

mediator. Someone who helps two groups or persons work out their differences and find a mutual solution. In the New Testament, Jesus is the only Mediator between God and the people of the earth.

Moabite. A native or resident of Moab, an ancient kingdom east of the Dead Sea. It is now known as Jordan.

money changers. An exchanger of coins, usually found with the people who sold items for use in the temples. If someone wanted to make an offering and needed non-Roman money, they took their currency to a money changer and traded it for non-Roman money. But it was not a free service. Some money changers were corrupt and did not trade fairly; they charged high fees and interest.

multitudes. Many of something of the same type, like a crowd of people.

myrhh. A sweet-smelling liquid that comes from certain small, spiny trees. It was used as both a perfume and a pain reliever. One of the wise men brought it as his gift to baby Jesus, and the merchants sold it on the caravan that bought Joseph.

Nazirite. A person who vowed to give up certain worldly things to dedicate oneself to God. Anyone could be a Nazirite—social or financial position in the community did not matter.

on high. In heaven. When Jesus talked about the "power from on high" (Luke 24:49), He was telling His followers that He had a job for them, but they were not to do it by themselves. Rather, they were to wait and God would give them the power to complete the job.

oppression. A physically or mentally cruel burden imposed by someone of authority.

overseer. A supervisor or manager; someone in charge.

Passover. A Jewish festival that celebrates when the Israelites were spared from the plague of Egypt, in which the firstborn of the Egyptians died. It was the first of three great festivals of the Hebrew people.

perceive. To understand or know.

perplexed. Puzzled or confused.

persecute. To harass, annoy, or trouble someone continually.

Pharisees. A Jewish religious and political party that strictly observed and kept the law of God as the scribes interpreted it.

Philistines. An aggressive group of people with a highly skilled military, and the main rivals of the Israelites. They lived in southwest Palestine in Old Testament times.

prodigal. Someone who is wasteful with their money.

prow. The front of a ship or boat, sometimes called the bow. The left front side would be the port bow or prow; the right front side would be the starboard bow or prow.

rebuke. To express disapproval of something that someone says or does.

revelation. Uncovering or disclosing. The way in which God sometimes makes Himself known to people.

rudder. A vertical blade located at the rear (stern) of a boat or ship which allows the boat or ship to change direction when it is moving.

Sabbath. The seventh day of the week, the day of rest for Israelites. It remembers the day God rested after creating the world. Christians observe Sunday as a day of rest like the Sabbath.

satrap. A governor of a region in the ancient Persian empire. He ruled on behalf of the emperor and had great authority.

seah. A dry measurement. One seah is one-third of an ephah. It is equal to 7 quarts or 7.3 liters.

seller of purple. A tradesperson who traded the dye "purple" and cloth colored by it. Purple was the rarest and therefore the most precious and expensive color of dye available. It took thousands of mollusks to make one ounce of purple dye. Lydia *(see Acts 16:14)* was a seller of purple dye and cloth.

shekel. A Hebrew weight of four-tenths of an ounce. It was also the name of a silver coin.

slaughter. To kill animals for food.

stern. The rear of a boat or ship.

tabernacle. The tent used by the Israelites as their sanctuary after the Exodus from Egypt until the temple was built; a house of worship.

taskmaster. Someone who assigns and closely supervises jobs. In biblical times, taskmasters were usually considered very cruel and harsh people who were the overseers of slave labor *(see overseer)*.

tongues. Languages. Someone who spoke many tongues spoke many languages.

unclean animal. Any animal that did not both chew the cud and have a cleft hoof, and could not be eaten.

vagabond. Someone without a home who wanders from place to place.

valor. Bravery or courage when facing danger.

vessel. Any type of boat or ship used to travel on water.

vexed. Irritated or annoyed.

wean. To remove a child from relying on its mother's milk. When a mother begins weaning her baby, she also begins feeding the child other food.

wilderness. An area like a forest or desert where only wild animals live; an area where it is difficult for people to survive within the natural surroundings.